Sandra,

I wish you maximum success!

Nathan
December 13, 2019

*"**The greatest aim of education is not knowledge but action.**"* ... Herbert Spencer

Live Debt Free

Live Debt Free

How to Build Your Road to Financial Independence

Nathan F. Dickerson

Nathan F. Dickerson

E-mail: MyDebtFreeTeam@Gmail.com

The purpose of this publication is to educate. All attempts have been made to verify provided information. This publication is not intended for use as a source of legal, accounting or other professional advice. All examples are hypothetical and for illustration purposes only.

ISBN 9781542392211

Dedicated to my wonderful wife, Phyllis, and our two remarkable daughters, Lynsie and Katelin. They give me incredible support, amazing understanding, remarkable patience and tremendous love.

My sincerest, life-long appreciation to Sherry Ridge, who on July 25th, 1996, literally changed my financial future. You shared your "Wisdom of the Ages" on how money works, how creditors work, and how, not only to become totally debt free; but more importantly, "what" living a debt free life would mean to having control of my financial future.

If I am to forever be indebted to anyone, it is to you, for the path you started me on to being debt free and financially independent.

To Gippy Graham who has always been there for me, even when he did not know it. Thanks "Coach" for your advice and wisdom as you encouraged me to "develop a philosophy on life."

"Soli Deo Gloria"

"Dripping water breaks a stone, not through force but through persistence." ... Ovid

Table of Contents

Foreword

I have been in the financial services industry since 2014. I've had the opportunity to lead an astounding team of advisors, who serve their clients in a fiduciary capacity, which enables our clients to meet their financial goals.

I'm married to the love of my life. We're on our own financial journey just like you, with all the ups and downs that come with it. In this book, you are going to read Nathan's story, as he shares his family's financial journey, and opens up his life. Nathan brilliantly uses his journey to show you how you can reach that point of financial freedom we all want to enjoy.

I've had the pleasure of knowing Nathan Dickerson for over 10 years at the time of this writing. My wish is that Nathan has received as much benefit from knowing me as I have from knowing him. I've never been in Nathan's presence that he hasn't left with me with something positive or beneficial, whether it be professionally or personally. He asked me to write this Foreword because he knows me both professionally and personally, and he knows that our goals align in our common interest of serving and helping others.

You are about to read a book by Nathan, shown through his eyes in the many extraordinary capacities he has positioned himself in throughout his life. Nathan, who I truly believe gets up every single day with one laser focused goal: Whose life can I help improve today? Nathan has worn many hats; a husband, a dad, a financial advisor, a coach, a leader, and a phenomenal motivator, just to name a few. The hat he never takes off is one that shows he truly and sincerely cares about people, and would rather make a positive impact in someone else's life, than to do something for himself.

I encourage you to read this book in its entirety. The path that Nathan is about to walk you down is a path he's been down himself. This isn't Nathan's opinions or speculation. These are mathematical facts, and he's put the math to the test for himself and others. Folks, this stuff works. If you're serious about improving your financial position, and deleting debt, the steps Nathan very clearly sets forth in this book will empower you to accomplish your goals.

Nathan's writing style in this book makes it a very easy read. It is written with simple language and doesn't require you to be a neurophysicist to comprehend the plan he sets forth.

Please read every word; twice. This is powerful stuff, yet so simple. If these steps were only applied by each household across the U.S. we would reduce the average household debt, increase the average household savings rate, and folks could retire earlier and more comfortably with less financial stress.

My hope is you receive as much value from reading this book as I have. Being in the financial services industry, my focus on a daily basis is on financial products, interest rates, gains, taxes, etc. It was a pleasant surprise to be reminded there really are simple, easy to apply steps that make a tremendous impact on one's financial future.

I wish you the very best in your journey. When you choose to follow what Nathan shares, I am confident your road will have fewer speed bumps and road blocks.

Micah H. Dixon

Associate Director
Investment Advisor Representative
Transamerica Financial Advisors, Inc.

Personal Message

What I have discovered, is that typically "it's not a question of income; it's a question of debt."

My goal is to provide information to help you understand how to design a strategy to become 100% debt free, and create a road map to build real wealth and financial independence!

In July 1996, my financial life changed due to the information I am going to share with you. The information holds as much value today, if not more, as it did then! I so appreciate the opportunity to share my story, and perspective, with you!

Throughout the book, I'll share with you a little about myself. Understand this is not "pie-in-the-sky" or "theory" about how to become debt free and financially independent. This is real; the knowledge I learned changed my financial life. More importantly, it may help you to change your financial life too.

And, when I say "financially independent" let me clarify my personal perspective. I believe you don't have to be "Rich" to be "Financially Independent." Everyone defines financial independence differently. For me, it means no one can put the squeeze on you and you are not a servant to the lender.

A Paradigm Shift – Live Debt Free:

1. You must make a commitment to yourself (and for your family).
2. You must control debt levels and understand how the credit industry works and how money works.
3. You must understand the financial impact of your home mortgage.
4. And, you must take action and have the desire and will to persevere.

My Paradigm Shift:

- I simply made a commitment to believe in myself. It was important as my family depended on me.
- I made sure to partner with my wife and my children, so we were all in alignment with our family goals.
- I learned about how debt can put us in financial jeopardy and about the unyielding power of creditors!
- I made a commitment to TAKE ACTION and to NEVER QUIT! I did not let anything, alter or influence me, nor did I listen to anyone who tried to tell me I was making a mistake, especially about paying off my mortgage, or that I would never be debt free!

As a result of following our plan, in just over six years, we became debt free; 100% debt free.

What is your six year personal vision? In six years you will arrive. Question is... where?

This is a real life application on how you can apply the information you are about to read and start on your road to living debt free and achieving financial independence; however you may personally define it.

Welcome to your new beginning!

Nathan Dickerson

 **Testimonials**

The information you are about to read has helped many people on their road to financial independence. Let me share a few of their personal testimonials as an encouragement that you too can live debt free.

"After considering the concepts in *"Live Debt Free"* the burden of debt shifted from being oppressive to a goal to be mastered. The simple tools for the elimination of debt are easily put into practice and I've already begun to see results. Our family's lifestyle is changing in healthy ways that fit our core beliefs about stewardship. Thank you for the challenge and the tools to put our financial resources to work for our future instead of working to pay off the past." BD... Minnesota

"At first I was angered by this information (at how creditors work); however, by the end, I wanted to start right away... I was empowered! I am now more aware of the power of creditors and will be more aware of what I do with my paycheck – so I can be sure it works for me. Now that's life changing information!" KJ... Ohio

"The principles in *"Live Debt Free"* are significantly and dramatically changing our lives because the basic truths set forth powerfully and effectively target the root of financial problems. We found this invaluable information easy to understand and to apply. It provides the necessary tools to help us gain better control of our finances. We have personally learned that it is not how much money we make that is important, but rather how we manage it. This information is life-changing and should be implemented by everyone!" PK... Kansas

Testimonials

"This book is amazing and life changing. I've read several debt free books. This is the first one that I could not stop reading and then read a second time. The information is clear and easy to understand. As I read the book it felt as if you and I were having a conversation and you were explaining the process. This allowed my family to organize our finances, understand how money works, and how creditors work. You helped us clearly understand and showed us the solution to becoming debt free. You have done an amazing job to help others and I highly recommend this book. This truly can change lives." LB... Kentucky

"I read your book two times so that I would absorb all of the information completely. The book has concise chapters that make it an easy read. Learning how to roll payments from one bill to the next in order to pay it off quicker is knowledge that everyone can understand and use. You have the ability to make the complex – simple." JD... North Dakota

"Recommend this book to all ages. Nathan articulates his successes to financial independence in clear, simple and common sense actions. The book is easy to follow, read and includes plenty of real life examples. Most of the world has accepted high interest rates and fees from credit card companies and banks... the reality clearly explained in his book is... why? This book motivates you to take charge of your finances and future... a must read! " PH... Florida

You have read from these testimonials how the information has helped others. Now, let's see how you can get started to Live Debt Free. Let's get started...

*"**Knowledge without action leads to self-delusion.**"* ... Dale Calvert

Chapter 1
"Ask 3 Questions"

One of my mentors is Dale Calvert.

Dale is a very successful entrepreneur, speaker, publisher, and home-based business professional. He has published numerous books, CDs, and has facilitated numerous trainings, both in person and on-line webinars, for multiple companies in the home-based business industry.

He is well respected for sharing "Wisdom of the Ages" and "Truths" about how to be successful.

I've had the opportunity to meet Dale in person, participate in many of his training webinars, and to attend one of his live training sessions.

There are many things I have learned from reading his books and listening to his CDs; to continuously focus on personal development being just one of them.

Dale's mentorship has been priceless to me.

One of the many things that I have learned, and use often, is Dale's "Ask 3 Questions."

What 3 Questions:
1) Who is this person?
2) What have they done?
3) Why should I listen to them?

Why are these questions important? Well, in one aspect, it's fairly simple.

Have you ever had someone "give you advice" or tell you "how to do something" and wanted you to listen to them?

So here is why these 3 questions become really important!

How do you know, that they know, what they are talking about? A lot of people want to tell you "how to" and have "never actually done" what they are prescribing that you should do! So, you can get to the truth of things pretty quickly by asking these 3 questions.

I've used these questions in my personal life and business life many, many times. Even at the expense of making it a little uncomfortable (sometimes for both them and for me)!

Let me share one example with you.

I spent 38 years in the corporate world. In one company (no, I cannot tell you who I worked for at that time), the training department brought in an "expert" to teach my leadership team (and me) about how to "coach" and "develop" the people who reported to us.

I was responsible for a team that oversaw and managed about 250 associates. As such, I was asked to participate in an initial meeting with this "expert" before their training started for our entire division.

During this meeting, the "expert" was telling me how best to "coach" my direct reports and "how to" best get maximum performance from them.

So, I asked the 3 questions:

1) Who is this person?
   ▶ Well, that was pretty easy to answer. I got the "family" and "places worked" types of answers.

2) What have they done?
   ▶ This is where it started to get interesting. What the individual had done was do "workshops" on "how to coach and develop" people.

3) Why should I listen to them?
   ▶ Here is the question I then asked of the person about "coaching" and "developing" people. And, that was, "How many teams have you personally managed, personally coached and developed?"

And the answer... "None." In other words, the "expert" had never before done, in a real life work application or setting, to personally "develop" or "coach" anyone.

Okay, it's time for a disclaimer. Let me be really clear about this. I'm not saying everyone has to have actually done something before they can teach on that topic. I get it. I do.

However, in this particular case, what was revealed to me, was that I did not want to "blindly" take the advice of this "expert" who had never before done what was about to be taught to my entire leadership team.

So, here is the point. **You should ask the 3 questions before considering the advice I present in this book.**

So, let me help answer them and to provide some insight for you. Why? I hope it will become evident:

1) Who is this person?
   - ▸ I'm pretty much like most people. I worked really hard to take care of my family and help raise our two daughters. I grew up in a single family household, my father passed when I was young, and my mother raised three kids on a church secretary's income. I put myself through college, even sold vacuum cleaners door to door, to pay for my senior year of school.

2) What have they done?
   - ▸ I talked about this earlier. When I met Sherry Ridge on July 25, 1996, I was on the same track as a lot of people. Two children, two cars (with 2 payments), credit cards (with on-going monthly payments), and 26 years left on my home mortgage. And, then, in just over 6 years I was totally, 100%, debt free.

3) Why should I listen to them?
   - ▸ I want to share with you "what I've done" and "how I've done it" and also give you some specific steps, and advice, so that you too, can be on a path to live debt free. This is "real-life" and not just something I want you to "blindly" follow. I've done it. You can too.

My goal is quite simple. I want to help you on your financial journey! I want to help you understand how to develop your debt elimination and wealth building plan. I want you to experience the benefits of not owing anything to anyone.

I want you to enjoy being able to pay cash for everything you want to purchase. I want you to be able to enjoy more of your personal time and to have more time with your family.

I want you to be able to better plan for your financial legacy; to give back, to provide, and to make a difference for others.

It's time to take action!

* * * * *

timea©123RF.com

Remember, "Ask 3 Questions"

Success is not always what some will make it seem.

Chapter 2
"My Story"

You never know who is going to come into your life, at any exact moment, and without knowing, have a dramatic impact. That happened to me on July 25, 1996.

Here's a bit of my story; it may help answer more of the 3 questions.

I think I'm pretty much like most people. Like most families, we all have things that happen in our life; some are good, some not so good. My dad passed when I was young. Mom then raised three kids on a church secretary's income. To be honest, looking back, I don't know how she did it. We didn't have much money but I never knew it. She managed to keep a roof over our head and food on the table. Mom was an incredible lady; she too has passed. Plus, I was born on her birthday; our birthday celebrations were amazing. She was always there for me. We had a special relationship!

From the time I was tall enough to stand behind a lawn mower, I was out working to make money. If I wanted any spending money I had to earn it. My first "real job" was working in a restaurant washing dishes. Then, I got to take food orders from customers. Yep, I was moving up! My very first customer order was for a bacon, lettuce, and tomato sandwich. I thought, how am I ever going to write all of that on this small order pad? Oh yeah, BLT. Interesting how these types of little things we just seem to always remember!

During high school, I worked every summer and, when it wasn't basketball season, I often worked after school and definitely on the weekends. Side note, I was a pretty good basketball player. Not a great player, though I did "letter" on the varsity team as a sophomore. And, I learned about "sticking it out" as we won some games and lost some games. But there I was as the only senior on the team. My coach had a lot to do with my perseverance; more on "The Coach" later.

Next challenge? College expenses. I worked to put myself through college.

To pay for my senior year of school, I sold vacuum cleaners, door-to-door, to cover that last year. (Don't think you can even sell door-to-door anymore). Bottom line, I did what it took to get it done. I was determined to make it. And, after having "average grades" in high school, I graduated from college "With Distinction" – something that I was (and still am) proud to have accomplished.

After school, I did like most people do. I got a job, a few years later; I got married, had two amazing children, and worked to make ends meet for my family. My wife was a teacher, and still is at the time of this writing, and teachers do not make a lot of money. At that time, I was in management in the retail world, and definitely was not making a ton of money. However, we made ends meet (for the most part), and we were raising our family.

In 1996, my daughters were young, and we lived in Gurnee, Illinois, which is about three miles south of the Wisconsin border. At that time, we had 2 cars, and 2 car payments. We had credit cards, and monthly credit card payments. And, we had 26 years left on our 30 year home mortgage.

‣ And, Then It Happened!

To help make ends meet, I joined a home-based business. Through that business I met Sherry Ridge, on July 25, 1996. My financial life would never be the same. I did not even come close to grasping, at that time, the impact Sherry, or what she taught me, would mean for my family.

The home-based business ended; however, what Sherry taught me; it changed our financial direction forever!

What Sherry taught me about is the "real business" creditors are in and what they want to take from us over our entire life. I learned how money works. I learned how mortgages work. I learned that if you don't know how your mortgage works, it has the potential, to significantly alter your financial future.

I learned that as we work hard for our money, we better position that money to work hard for us. I learned that $1.00 goes a lot further, if you don't owe anything to anyone, than $1.00 goes if you owe $5.00.

I also learned that you don't have to be rich to be financially independent. People define being "financially independent" many ways. Let's take a couple of minutes and let me share these two perspectives with you.

Contentment: What I have learned over the years is that having "contentment" and appreciating the many blessings in my life has been very beneficial on my financial journey.

Learning to be content helped me to not pursue "keeping up with the Jones family" and not needing to have the biggest house in the neighborhood or to drive the fanciest car.

We live in a modest home; and I am content in my dwellings. Here is one example, of the real power of the information, you are about to read in this book. By my family following the information; just one of the many things it did for us was, when we moved into our modest home; we paid cash.

Broke at a higher level: I have known people who have made "a lot" of money. I've known people who have made a "modest" amount of money.

It's not always about how much money you make. It's about not spending every dollar you make! It's about being smart with the dollars you do make.

I've had people tell me the only reason they have a high level of debt is because they have a high level of income. In my working with many people, I have seen, time after time after time; it's not a question of income... it's a question of debt.

Don't be broke at a higher level.

Start a journey to re-define **"normal"** for your family.

By re-defining normal, my family, in just over 6 years, went from having 2 car payments, credit card payments, and a 30 year mortgage, to being debt free! Yes, even our 30 year mortgage was paid off. And, we did it using only the money we made at our regular jobs. We did not inherit any money and we did not find a pot of gold at the end of the rainbow.

Following, are what we learned, what we took action upon, and what I hope, will help you, to live debt free.

* * * * *

"Normal is getting dressed in clothes that you buy for work and driving through traffic in a car that you are still paying for – in order to get to the job you need to pay for the clothes and the car, and the house you leave vacant all day so you can afford to live in it."

... Ellen Goodman

Chapter 3
"Begin With The End In Mind"

Stephen R. Covey, in his book, "*The Seven Habits of Highly Effective People,*" emphasizes the principle that we should "*begin with the end in mind.*"

So let's begin with the end in mind. Imagine that you are totally debt free. You have no car payments. No credit card debts. And, you have no home mortgage debt. You pay cash for everything. You are investing your money and building real wealth. You are able to do the things you want and when you want. Can it happen? Absolutely!

In just over a 6 year period, by implementing the following concepts, my family and I became 100% debt free. What I learned in the process, is that no one has to wait until retirement age to be debt free. Let me emphasize again that during this time, we did not win the lottery, or inherit any money, or get a second or third job. We did however; discover a legitimate path to financial independence using just the money earned from our regular jobs.

> ▶ **You can be on your road to total financial independence starting – TODAY!**

As I reflect on my life and educational experiences, it is disheartening to realize that I and many of my contemporaries were not adequately taught how money works. Parents seldom teach their children this information, not due to neglect; it was simply not included in the curriculum in many schools. Most people go through life never having been taught about spending, cash flow, credit management, interest income, interest expense, or how loans and mortgages really function.

So what are the sources from which we receive our financial education?

Well, what do we see on TV? Our cell phones? How about what we read in all the popular magazines? Aren't we constantly faced with the pressures of keeping up with the Jones, the "I must have it now" syndrome, and the emphasis on the status level one is expected to achieve? We are bombarded daily from every angle; magazines, newspapers, TV, and the Internet.

The problem is, in most cases, no one ever taught us to understand the value and management of money. No one shared with us how creditors drain the financial life right out of us as we succumb to their never-ending bombardment of advertising and temptation pressures.

The bottom line is that we must think for ourselves. We have been told, from primarily the creditors, WHAT to think for way too long. We are told to follow "their" conventional wisdom, we are told to "color within the lines," we are told to get a job and keep it for 40 years. Then what do we end up with?

▸ **Well, 95% of us retire flat broke.**

It's time to think differently!

Isn't financial independence, and to live debt free, what we all desire for ourselves and for our family? To do more of what we want, and when we want? Wouldn't you like to be more in control of how you spend your time; valuable time to spend with your family and time for yourself?

How can we experience financial freedom if we are living paycheck to paycheck, even if those paychecks are really substantial? Can one be truly free if, every day and every night, he or she is filled with financial worry?

Being in debt – what does it mean to you?

- ▸ Missing opportunities?
- ▸ Being impacted by the economy?
- ▸ Increased stress levels with impacts to your family, health, marriage?
- ▸ Being incapable of sufficiently investing to build for your retirement?
- ▸ Being vulnerable to a company?

How do you answer these questions? Have you experienced these various challenges by being in debt? Are you ready to break free and never miss another opportunity and never be vulnerable to a company again? To a terrible boss again?

It is by no accident that you have made the decision to study and understand this life-changing information. Nor is it by luck or by chance. The reason you have this valuable information today, is the result of your vision, passion, and determination to better position your overall financial future!

- ▸ **I commend you on this important decision, because it is in your moments of decision that your destiny is shaped.**

Our goal, our mission, is to help you! Today is a new day for you! Today you start on your road to live debt free!

From our information, you will:

1) Learn how money works and how to make it to work hard for you

2) Understand how creditors want to literally take every penny of your future earnings and how you can stop them in their tracks

3) Discover the plain and simple truth about how your mortgage really works

4) Discover why you must control your debt level

5) Be able to determine your debt freedom date

    a) No car payments

    b) No credit card payments

    c) No home mortgage

6) Realize what is your most valuable asset

7) Learn how to use this knowledge to become totally debt free, including paying off your home mortgage, and how to do it in the shortest period of time, and

8) Learn how to turn money that was formerly used for debt payments into wealth-generating income leading to being debt free and financially independent.

▸ **And, to start this process – NOW!**

Our goal is to help you take control of your financial life, free yourself from the bondage of debt, and the destruction it has over people. So that you are in control of your time! So that you are able to do what you want and when you want!

We want to help design your debt free life to enjoy time with your family! We want you to live again... dream again... have more control of your life again!

In these changing economic times, what are some of the serious challenges people are facing today? Understand that you're not alone in this current state; however, it can change.

What is keeping people from dreaming again and from having more control of their financial life?

Let's review a few shocking statistics:

- ▶ "Over 70% of workers say they are living paycheck to paycheck." — Bankrate.com

- ▶ "Over 60% of workers said their debt is a problem." — Employee Benefit Research Institute Retirement Survey

- ▶ "Approximately 60% of workers have less than $25,000 in retirement investments." — Employee Benefit Research Institute Retirement Survey

- ▶ "Total outstanding student loan balance stands at about $1.2 trillion." — Consumer Financial Protection Bureau

- ▶ "People 60 and over are carrying nearly $66 billion in student loan debt." — Consumer Financial Protection Bureau

- ▶ "A majority, or 69%, of Americans don't have enough cash on hand to handle a $1,000 emergency." — GOBanking Rates Survey

- ▶ "If one paycheck were late, 61% of respondents in a survey said they were concerned about not having enough to cover every day expenses." — Pew Charitable Trusts Report

And we wonder why 95% are in a serious financial situation. It is important to define your plan to become 100% debt free and financially independent.

So, ask yourself these important questions as you read the information being presented to you:

1) Do these financial concepts make sense?

2) Do I have a personal plan to:
   - Protect my current income?
   - Eliminate my debts?
   - Live debt free?
   - Build my retirement income?

3) If I put these concepts into practice, would I be better off?

4) On a scale of 1 – 10 (1 being low and 10 being high); what is my desire to live debt free and to be financially independent?

As you understand the answers to these questions, especially number 4, then you can start on your plan to being debt free and financially independent!

For these reasons, I will review 5 money concepts and how to apply them so you can achieve your goals:

- ▶ **Concept 1 – Millionaires in the Making**

- ▶ **Concept 2 – The Power of Compound Interest**

- ▶ **Concept 3 – Present and Future Value of Money**

- ▶ **Concept 4 – How to Systematically Eliminate and Payoff all Your Debts, and**

- ▶ **Concept 5 – How to Achieve True Financial Independence**

Before we review these five concepts individually, let me begin with the "end in mind" for you. I have a passion to share this valuable and powerful information with you so that you experience similar blessings – Live Debt Free!

I am blessed with time and freedom to enjoy life with my family. I am the one who decides if I work, not my creditors.

However, it's not always been that way for me. When I was younger, no one ever taught me how money really works.

Sad, but true!

Generally, as mentioned earlier, money management information is not taught in schools, nor is it taught in the work place, nor by most parents, as evidenced by 95% of people retiring broke (more on this later), and it surely is not taught by the mortgage and credit card industries!

So, what changed?

Fortunately, I was introduced to the concepts that I will share with you. Concepts, coupled with understanding and with taking action, which allowed my financial life to take on new meaning – take on new hope – take on renewed energy – and take on incredible optimism.

> **I was literally so excited that I could not sleep!**

Realize what I am saying: I went from owing everything to every creditor; to in just over 6 years, using only the money I was making from my regular job, to being 100% debt free!

All of these things did not change overnight. However, I was on a new direction. I had set a new course for my family.

> **If I can do it – so can you!**

Let's get you started on your new direction to live debt free!

* * * * *

"You must get good at one of two things: planting in the spring or begging in the fall."

... Jim Rohn

Chapter 4
"Financial Planning Guideline – An Overview"

There are financial planning guidelines that you need to be aware of as you move forward. These guidelines will help ensure you are addressing key points.

Everyone is in a unique and different financial position; you are in a unique and different financial position. As such, there is not a way to give you ALL the specifics for your personal plan; however, this guideline will give you a great overview.

Why?

Because; planning, is not One-Size-Fits-All. Don't let anyone tell you that it is. There are enough "experts" on TV all trying to sell a one-size-fits-all approach. They do this so they can appeal to the masses. They know if they cover with a wide brush stroke they will get enough people who will buy whatever it is they are selling.

▶ When it comes to your plan it needs to be "Your Plan."

What I can tell you, which will benefit you tremendously, is what you need to consider and know, that should be your "Financial Planning Guideline."

Here would be a good place for you to say, "Hey, Nathan, what about those 3 questions I should be asking?" Great point; it's what I'd do if I were you.

I've done financial coaching for people and designed specific debt-elimination strategies based on their financial position. At the beginning of this book, you read testimonials from people I have worked with to help them with their personal debt-elimination plan.

What I've not shared with you, up to this point, is that after getting out of the corporate rat race after 38 years; I was an investment representative and financial coach for a major Fortune 500 financial services company.

I always wanted to take my passion for helping people on their financial journey to the next level. So, after earning a life insurance license, and earning 4 securities licenses, I was able to fulfill this passion. I can share with you that I had numerous clients that I worked with and in all areas of their financial life.

So, with that as a background, let me share key points as a "Guideline Overview" in what you need to consider, and factor in for "Your Plan" as you start to Live Debt Free.

Financial Guideline:

1) Follow the debt elimination and wealth building plan as illustrated throughout this book.
   - There is harmony, peace, and less stress to Live Debt Free; experience it.

2) Do not spend more than you make.
   - Check your spending to keep a positive cash flow. Don't have more "month left over" at the end of your "money." Have more money left over at the end of the month.

3) Do not be a financial slave to the lender.
   - Control your debt levels as you work to Live Debt Free. In other words, don't let creditors master over you.

4) Fortify your current financial position.
   - You should have six months of living expenses as an emergency fund. If you're not there yet, work towards saving a minimum of six months.

5) Safeguard your future earning power.
- Have the right financial products in place to continue your income should you get sick or injured and cannot work. Your debts will continue to roll in even if your income stopped. Make sure you safeguard your future earnings.
- Have the right amount of life insurance in place, to continue your income for your family, as we never know when we will be called Home.

6) Establish your long-term goals.
- As you eliminate your debts, put monies into savings for your retirement.
- Put monies into savings for educational needs or other savings goals.
- Put monies into savings to enjoy life.

7) Build your retirement nest egg.
- At retirement the key is to have a monthly guaranteed income that you can never out live.

8) Be content with all you are creating for your family.
- Be a blessing to others.

Some of these points you'll want to start on immediately and others will occur over the long term. However, as you start to eliminate your debts, you will be able to use this Guideline as a roadmap to serve in your overall personal plan. This will also give you things to talk about if, or when, you work with a trained financial coach and planner. Keep these in mind as you continue reading.

Now, let's start your journey to Live Debt Free!

* * * * *

"You cannot change your destination overnight, but you can change your direction overnight." ... Jim Rohn

Chapter 5
"Millionaires in the Making"

To begin this journey, you must first understand:

Concept 1 – Millionaires in the Making

The typical person produces a lot of money in their lifetime.

According to Federal Reserve, at the time of this writing, the median household income in the United States was $56,516. Now this number could be a little more or a little less where you live, but the median is $56,516. Take that number and multiply it by the 40 years most people spend working.

Those 40 years will produce income of $2,260,640.

The typical person is a millionaire in the making. How much are you on track to make in your lifetime? Do the math.

With this in mind, what then is your most valuable asset?

When this question is asked, people often respond with answers like their boat, their car, and most often, their house. However, as you see from the above income of over 2.2 million dollars, your most valuable asset is definitely "income generation."

Yes, your ability to produce an income is your greatest asset. It allows you to pay off your debts, build your wealth, and secure the financial future for you and for your family.

With the obvious importance of an on-going income for your family, and to provide for their financial future, would you agree... you should protect your 2.2 million dollar income?

▶ Protect your future income earnings for your family.

In other words, protect your future income, should something happen to you, through the proper type of life insurance.

Now this topic might not be what you first expected you would hear talked about. However, should something happen to you, your family will need a source of income to keep food on the table, to pay the mortgage, the car, the credit cards, and to pay for your children's education.

Why do I bring this topic up to you? Let me share a statistic that is a disaster waiting to happen for families:

▶ **"42% of Americans have no life insurance."**
— Bankrate Money Pulse Survey

As you build wealth, which takes time, you must protect your income. You are your greatest income generating asset! Without your income, or without providing for the continuation of your income through the proper type and amount of life insurance, your family could be left in a financial disaster.

If this topic has not been properly addressed, by you and your family, then it needs to be done with a sense of urgency.

Now, what does happen to all that money you generate over your working life?

If you are going to make an average of about 2.2 million dollars, what happens to all your money? Where does it all go? And why, according to the Department of Health and Human Services, out of 100 people who start working a 40 year career at the age of 25, by the age of 65, why are only 5% financially well-off? What happened to the other 95%?

Believe me; I am not making up the following numbers.

On average, for every 100 people after a 40 year career, the following outcomes would exist at age 65:

- 1% will be considered wealthy

- 4% will have adequate capital

- 18% will still be working

- 61% are dependent on Social Security, friends, relatives, or charity

- 16% are deceased

▸ **According to this particular study, 95% are either dead or dead broke.**

People don't plan to fail… they fail to plan. At retirement, only 5% are considered to be financially independent. My question to you is which group do you want to be in? The 95% who are dead or dead broke? Or, the 5% who are financially secure?

You may ask, where did their average 2.2 million dollars go?

What really happened to all their money? Didn't they work hard all their life, so why do only 5% achieve financial independence? How does this happen?

Well, I would venture to say they had:

1) No Financial Education

2) No Financial Game Plan

3) No Financial Coach

4) No Understanding of the Real Business of Creditors

5) No Control Over Spending too Much; Saving too Little

Even the greatest of athletes have a coach. And, even the greatest of our national leaders have advisors (coaches). With this information not being taught in schools, wouldn't you agree, that we all can use a financial coach?

Let the information in this book be a "Financial Coach." Let it help you develop a "Financial Game Plan." Take action from what's presented and get that – Debt Monkey – off your back.

People work hard for their money, but they never get their money to work hard for them!

Why? As previously stated, no one ever taught them how!

There are also 3 fatal mistakes that keep people from ever getting their money to work for them. Let's explore them in the next chapter.

Chapter 6
"The Most Powerful Force In The Universe"

Fatal Mistake Number 1 - Spend Don't Save

Okay, this chapter is short, sweet and fairly obvious; however, it's more than just saying "I didn't save for a rainy day."

Yes, part of why 95% of the people end up financially drained is that they spend all their money and never save; however, that really just scratches the surface of the real problem.

I'll save starting "later" is nothing but a financial disaster in the making. As for most people, "later" usually never comes; but too often, the disaster still manages to show up!

As mentioned earlier, too many people spend all they make. And it sometimes doesn't matter if they make a lot of money or a little money. If more, I've seen many times; they are broke at a higher level. Don't spend every dime you make.

Now, let's take a look at how money works. Let's begin to get your money working for you!

Concept 2 – The Power of Compound Interest

What is compound interest? Well, simply put, it is interest being paid on interest. In other words, after interest is paid to you in one month on your savings total, that new higher total now earns even more interest the next month.

Interest paid on interest. Is it very powerful? Absolutely!

Albert Einstein recognized as one of the most intelligent men of all time, when asked what he considered to be the most powerful force in the universe answered: **"Compound interest!"**

Let's look at three examples:

▶ Ron is 30 years old. He saves $166 per month, about $5.50 per day, and does so until he reaches age 65. If he earns 6% interest, by age 65 he will have $237,684. Ron saved approximately $70,000 over those 35 years. Compound interest grew his money to over $237,000.

▶ Pam is 20 years old. She saves $400 per month and does so for 30 years achieving a 10% rate of return. By age 50, Pam will have $911,730. Pam saved a total of $144,000. Compound interest has grown her money to over $900,000.

▶ Mary is 25 years old. She saves $325 per month and does so until retirement at age 65. Mary only saved during this time a total of $156,000. If Mary gets 8% interest, by age 65, she will have $1,142,141.

The Power of Compound interest made Mary a MILLIONAIRE.

In one's lifetime, roughly 2.2 million dollars is generated. Let's see where things really stand. If Mary saved, as in the example, she would accumulate over $1 million at retirement.

So why do 95% of the people end up without adequate financial resources? Look at the potential income and note the examples listed about how compound interest can literally put thousands of dollars into your pocket; if you get your money to work hard for you.

What is keeping people from taking advantage of the power of compound interest?

Keep reading to learn more on how money works and how to get money to work for you!

* * * * *

Chapter 7
"Creditors! Are You Giving Them All Your Money?"

Fatal Mistake Number 2 – Creditors Taking All Your Money

Yes, creditors want all your money, and in 95% of the cases, they succeed.

Let me say this again, creditors want, and often get, every penny you make.

Why are they able to succeed at this? Because they do not have your best interest at heart. Because they understand how money works. Because they fully understand the power of compound interest. Because they understand that if you DO NOT KNOW how money works, then they can get your money to work for them and not for you.

Why?

> ▶ **Because Creditors Are In The Business Of Making Money – YOUR MONEY!**

I will tell you this – creditors want all the money you will make in your lifetime. They want every penny of the 2.2 million dollars you are going to make. And you know what's sad; they get it in 95% of the cases.

How does this happen you ask? Let's explore three major purchases we make as consumers:

1) Our homes

2) Our cars, and

3) All the various items we buy using credit cards

Our focus is on building your road to live debt free.

We will cover all three major questions:

- ▸ Have a mortgage?
- ▸ Have car payments?
- ▸ Maxed out on credit cards?

Allow me to ask you this first question.

Do you understand how your mortgage really works?

Don't worry if you don't. If your answer is "no" you are in the majority.

However, here is an essential question you must understand:

- ▸ **Is Your Mortgage Destroying Your Financial Future?**

Most people do not know how their mortgage works. Most people do not understand how mortgage interest works. And unfortunately, most people's financial future is being significantly impacted by their mortgage (or actually, the lack of knowledge around how their mortgage really works).

So, today, let's fix this understanding for you!

Let's use an example of a $200,000 home mortgage, for a 30 year period, at 7% interest. Your monthly mortgage payment, which includes principal and interest on this home, is $1,330.60. See the amortization table on page 124.

Here is a graph showing your normal 30 year payout schedule. This shows the purchase price in the top left corner of $200,000. It then shows the balance by every other year; ending at zero after thirty years.

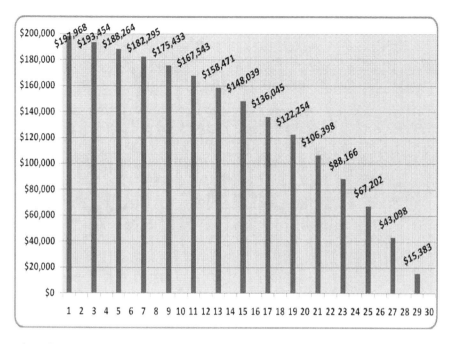

The fundamental question is how much, over the life of the 30 year mortgage, does this $200,000 house really cost?

Well, the real cost of this home is $479,021.94. Simply take the principal and interest payment of $1,330.60 and multiply by 360 payments. (30 years X 12 months = 360 payments plus a final payment adjustment of $5.94).

You have paid almost 240% of the original price of your home. You will have paid over $279,000 in interest! See the amortization table on page 135.

▶ **Your $200,000 home costs you $479,021**

Look closely at this (and fully understand) what is happening. The mortgage company is taking your compound interest earning power away from YOU so that THEY can keep almost all of YOUR money.

In our example, here is how your first monthly payment breaks down. Remember, your monthly mortgage payment, which includes both principal and interest, is $1,330.60. Of this total, only $163.93 goes towards paying off your principal. That means you are paying $1,166.67 in interest. See the amortization table, payment 1, on page 124.

Over 87% of your payment is going towards interest.

As a matter of fact, in the first 12 months alone, you will have paid a total of $15,967.20 in payments. Of this amount, $13,935.65 is interest. Which means only $2,031.55 actually goes toward paying down your loan amount. Do you grasp how the money tables are being turned totally against you?

This graph below shows principal and interest by month for your first 12 months. Is this eye-opening or what?

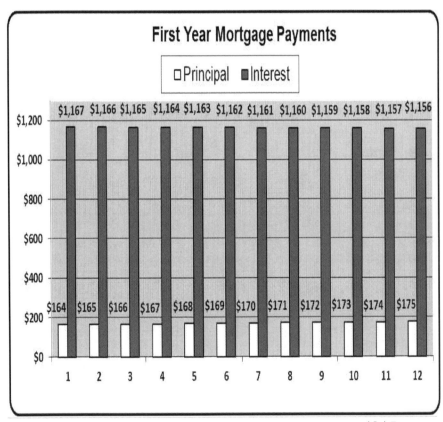

Recap – Year One Mortgage Payment:

- ▸ Total Payments: $15,967
- ▸ Total Interest: $13,935
- ▸ Total Principal: $2,032
- ▸ Year One Interest: 87%

For year one totals, see the amortization table on page 124.

And, in this mortgage example, this is just the beginning of the 7% mortgage loan!

For most people, their mortgage is their single largest purchase. It's important to know the "details" of exactly how your mortgage works.

As you can see, in the beginning years, your mortgage payment is primarily interest. Then in the later years, your payment goes proportionately more to the principal.

However, it's vital to understand these details of how your mortgage is actually structured by the mortgage lender.

Why?

Because this knowledge will empower you to make more informed decisions on how it's best to pay off your mortgage in the quickest time period possible!

Note: The actual interest rates used in the various examples throughout the book, may be more than or may be less than, what's actually happening in the marketplace today. Do not focus on the actual rates used – **understand the concept.** That's the key. Grasp the concept as rates always change.

Keep reading! There's a lot more to learn about mortgages.

* * * * *

Chapter 8
"The Plain And Simple Truth About How Your Mortgage Works"

Fatal Mistake Number 3 – Mortgage Interest Pitfalls

When you got your mortgage, did you say? "Hallelujah, the bank "approved me" for a loan so they can have a significant part of my financial life for the next 30 years!" Really, 30 years just to pay off your home mortgage? Feel trapped?

But wait! "I own my home!" you say. Or, do you?

If you think you own your home, just stop making your mortgage payments for about 6 months and see who really owns your home!

No one owns their home unless they have it totally paid off. However, you absolutely do not have to have a mortgage for 30 years or even for 15 years!

Once you understand the "plain and simple truth" about how your mortgage works, trust me, you will want to pay it off as quickly as possible.

Why would anyone want to consciously lock up 30 years of their financial future? You do not have to as you are about to learn!

Before we get into more of the actual specifics of how your mortgage works, let's first discuss some basics of how money works. This will be vital to your overall understanding of ensuring you are on a path to live debt free.

You work hard for your money. I want you to understand how to get your money to work hard for you!

Let's say you buy a home with a 7%, 30 year, mortgage.

Did your mortgage lender say you were getting a 7% interest loan? Well, it would be 7% if you paid the entire loan off in your first year. However, we know that isn't happening. So when we say, "I thought the mortgage broker told me I got a 7% loan," well, all we have to do is the math.

And, if the first year concerns you – stay tuned.

When I began on my road to live debt free, this discovery was my first big "ah-ha" moment. When I realized almost 90% of my mortgage payment at that time was interest and how much I was going to pay for my home, I knew I had to take a different course of action.

> ▶ **As author Mark Caine said, "The first step toward success is taken when you refuse to be a captive of the environment in which you first find yourself."**

I did not like the reality of being a captive. Yes, I knew it was time to think differently; time to make a paradigm shift.

Let me ask you this. Have you ever moved your family into a new residence? According to the National Association of Realtors, people move on average every 7 years. With this in mind, let's keep reviewing more facts about your mortgage.

After 7 years of making your $1,330.60 in monthly payments, by how much have you lowered your principal? After all, you have paid 7 years of your 30 year mortgage.

So seven years would be a total of 84 payments (7 years x 12 months). In those 84 payments of $1,330.60, you would have made total payments in the amount of $111,770.40.

At this point, of that $111,770 in payments (and you will not like this), only $17,705 went to lowering your principal.

Yes, after 7 years, you still owe $182,295, or over 90%, of your original $200,000 mortgage. The amount of interest you have already paid is staggering. See the amortization table, payment 84, on page 126.

For every time you move, or for every time you refinance your home – you start over again at paying virtually nothing but interest on your mortgage payments!

CAUTION! You will see tons of advertising to refinance your home; all pitching to lower your monthly payment. However, it may not be in your best interest. You have to consider how many years you've had your current mortgage and how much you've already paid in interest. And, how many payments do you have left to make on your mortgage.

Then, more importantly (and this is critical), you have to look at how much of your future payments will go to paying off principal. You may have a greater amount of those future payments paying off principal and less going to interest. You may be closer to paying off your mortgage than your realize.

Assuming a person moves three times in their life, and at the 7 year average, then for 21 years they are paying virtually only interest on their home. I've known many people in their 50's that still have 20 years or more to pay on their mortgage.

What is your situation after making 15 years of payments?

Surely after paying 15 years of your 30 year mortgage, 180 payments, you have paid off 50% of the loan. Well, after 15 years, you still owe $148,039! After 15 years, you still owe roughly 75% of your original $200,000 amount. See the amortization table, payment 180, on page 129.

Well, if your 30 year mortgage is not 50% paid off after 15 years, then when? How many years does it take for your 30 year mortgage to be paid to the 50% level?

The answer, quite sadly, is on payment number 261. See the amortization table, payment 261, on page 132.

See the chart below of your normal 30 year payout. Yes, your mortgage is 50% paid off at 21 years and 9 months!

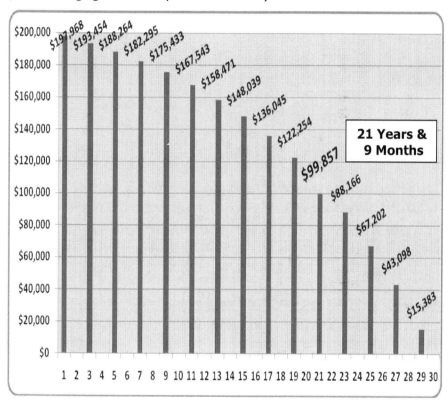

Recap – 30 Year Mortgage 50% Paid Off:

▸ Year 21 and 9 Months
▸ Principal Balance: $99,857
▸ Total Payments: $347,286
▸ Total Interest: $247,144

Do you grasp what is happening with your money?

Your 30 year mortgage is 50% paid off just short of 22 years. WOW! Plus – the total interest you've paid is $247,144 (and remember the purchase price was $200,000).

> ▶ **If you get nothing else from reading this book, other than gaining the knowledge of how your mortgage works – it will be worth <u>THOUSANDS</u> of dollars to you!**

Are you starting to see the picture? Are you starting to see what is really happening to your earning power? Starting to see how, in these examples, people can never get to the point of having their money work for them?

However, here is the good news, beginning today, all of that can change for you! So stay tuned, but for the time being let's stay on the path of learning.

In our example, by the time you have completely paid off your 30 year home loan, you will have paid the $200,000 original cost plus $279,021 in interest, for that grand total of $479,021. And it gets worse. You see you need $479,021 of actual, in-your-pocket dollars, to make the payments.

What does that mean? That means, assuming you are in the 25% tax rate bracket, you will have to earn approximately $638,700 over those 30 years, to be able to pay roughly $159,675 (25% of $638,700) in state and federal taxes alone, to have the $479,021, so that you can pay the $279,021 in interest, plus your original $200,000 loan. WHEW...

Think about what is really happening as this is your money!

Day 1: You've purchased your new home, started your new job – and you realize you have to earn $638,700 over the next 30 working years – just to pay the total cost of your $200,000 home.

And, this only covers the principal and interest. We haven't said anything about property insurance, property taxes, and repairs and upkeep; let alone, all the other "life's expenses." That money has to come out of the income too.

See what's happening to your money? And people wonder, "How is it I made all this money, and now that I'm retiring, I have very little money for myself and for my family?"

CAUTION! What about your tax deduction? My accountant (when I had a mortgage) said to me, "Do not pay off your house, you'll lose your tax deduction!" I said to him, "So you think it's better for me to give the mortgage company $1.00 in interest, so the government can give me back 25 cents on my tax return? Isn't it better that I just KEEP my 75 cents?"

He said, "I've never thought about it that way." And, he was an accountant doing what he had always done because it had always been done that way. It's time to think differently!

Don't let these things happen to you; think differently! I will show you how to eliminate your debts in concept number four.

* * * * *

aleutie©123RF.com

Chapter 9
"Fast Track Your Mortgage Payoff"

Let's explore the value of $1.00 per day. Over a month, what is the value to you of one less latte coffee, one less soda, one less bagel, one less fast food lunch, or one less pizza?

As this "one less $1.00 per day" adds up to $30.00 a month, how can you use this to Fast Track your mortgage payoff? If you apply this extra $30.00 each month on your mortgage principal, what impact does it have on paying off your 30 year mortgage sooner?

This chart shows total savings of 2 years and 1 month by Fast Tracking payments each month of $30.00.

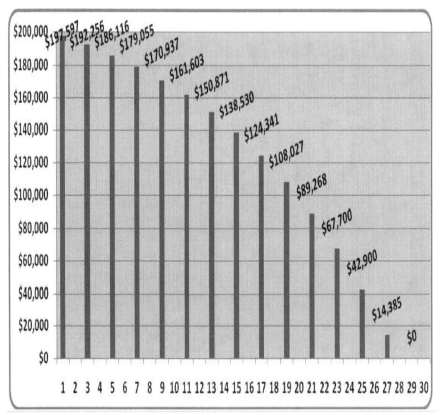

Yes, making one additional $30.00 payment on your mortgage each month saves you over 2 years of payments and $23,296.

Recap – Mortgage Payoff - $30 Fast Track:

▸ $30 Per Month: Additional Principal Payment

▸ Reduce Mortgage: 2 Years and 1 Month

▸ Total Savings: $23,296

As illustrated, $1.00 a day, $30.00 per month, can save you thousands on your mortgage! Would that be worth one less pizza each month and a few less cups of latte coffee?

But what happens as you are able to eliminate more debt? How can you best position those dollars to also impact your financial life? How can you speed up paying off your mortgage?

What if you eliminated monthly debt payments totaling $470?

▸ Eliminate your car payment

▸ Eliminate your credit card debt

▸ Eliminate your personal bank loan

▸ Eliminate your department store debt

▸ Eliminate mortgage second line of credit debt

What if you eliminated $470 of monthly debts?

What impact could an extra $470 per month have on the payoff of your $200,000 mortgage?

This chart on the next page shows the total savings of 15 years off your 30 year mortgage by Fast Tracking payments each month of $470.

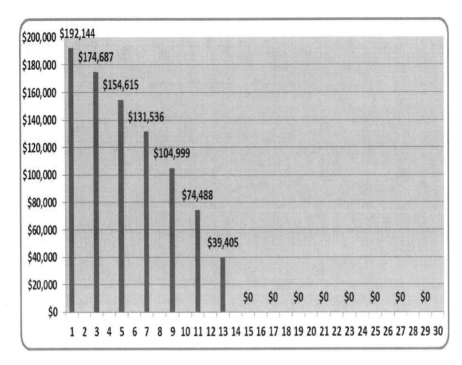

Yes, making an additional $470 payment each month on your mortgage saves you 15 years of payments and $155,847.

> ▸ **You would pay off your home in just 15 years!**

Recap – Mortgage Payoff - $470 Fast Track:

- ▸ $470 Per Month: Additional Principal Payment
- ▸ Reduce Mortgage: 15 Years and 0 Months
- ▸ Total Savings: $155,847

For now (we will come back to mortgages later), let's move on to discuss the second of the three creditors that want all your money; your car loan.

It's the same as with your house payment. They want as much of your money as <u>YOU</u> will give to them.

* * * * *

Chapter 10
"How Much Is That New Car?"

Let me share another story with you. I will call this one, **"Coming from a position of strength."**

Both my daughters worked summer jobs during school and experienced learning about the value of a dollar. We supported them when it came to big purchases. Like a car.

When it was time to get our daughters a car, our strategy was that I would co-sign for the car to help them establish credit. Then, after making payments for six months, we would pay off the car; which is exactly what we did.

After my youngest daughter had picked out her car at the dealership, yes, the car was two years old; we were then sitting in front of the finance person to set up payment terms.

After completing the paperwork, the finance person slid the forms in front of my daughter and said, "That will be 3.99% interest, sign here."

▶ **Wait one minute!**

Up to this point, my daughter handled most of the process. After all, this was a life-learning experience. When your debt is in control, **you can come from a position of strength.**

So, I said to the finance person, "No, that interest rate is not acceptable. I know my credit rating." So, with a somewhat bewildered look on her face, she said, "let me take another look at it" and by golly, she did.

In the final set of terms, after being able to stand firm, my daughter signed her payment terms at... 1.99% interest!

Position yourself to come from a position of strength. It will allow you to have more control over your money and over your creditors; another benefit of being debt free.

Now, here is what happens way too often. You buy a new car, drive it off the lot, and it drops in value from basically just pulling off the lot. This is why I don't recommend buying brand new cars. It's best to look for 2 to 4 year old models as it saves hundreds, if not thousands, of dollars.

So, with your new car, did the salesperson say to you, "Your payment is only $452 a month?" Yes, for only 60 months at just 5%. "Not a problem" you say, "I can afford that right along with my $1,330 a month house payment."

So that new shiny car with a $24,000 sticker price, after making 60 payments with interest, now costs you $27,175. So at this point, you are actually paying 113.23% for the not so new 5 year old car! And, having said that, you may also be upset, realizing you paid $27,175 for your $24,000 car.

However, if you had paid cash for the car, took the $3,175, (difference between $27,175 and $24,000), and invested it at 8% interest for the same 60 months you would have made car payments, the $3,175 would have grown to $4,730. And this $4,730 would then be in your savings account!

Sometimes, it's the little steps like this, which can make you money. So not only did that car cost you $27,175 it also cost you $4,730 in lost savings. Oh, and the average value for this 5 year old car: $9,600. So much for having bought a new car for only $24,000. However, this is just the beginning!

Think about this question. How many years have you had a car payment? I once had a boss who said to me, "I will always have a car payment." And, he probably did; and in doing so "literally drove" his financial future right to the car scrap heap. My point is; a lot of people have a car payment for most all their life!

So then what really happens?

If you had a car payment of $452 for 25 years, you'd spend a total of $135,600 in payments! And, if this isn't bad enough, had you invested the $452 over those 25 years at an 8% return... your money would have accumulated to... $432,730.

You can put your money into new cars; or, you can put your money to work for you. So, again I ask, what is your new car really costing you? Creditors will give you up to 6 years, or even longer, to pay off your car. Why? Because the longer you make payments, the more of your money they get!

▶ **It's no more complicated than that.**

Having mentioned credit rating let me share that the Fair Credit Reporting Act requires each of the 3 credit reporting agencies: Equifax, Experian and TransUnion, to provide to you a FREE credit report, at your request, once every 12 months.

At the time of this writing, Equifax, Experian and TransUnion use one website and phone number to order your free annual credit report; so, you don't need to contact them individually.

To order your free annual credit report:
▶ Phone: 1-877-322-8228
▶ Website: www.AnnualCreditReport.com

Note: You can order your free credit report from the 3 agencies at the same time; however, you may stagger them throughout the year providing you with a periodic review.

Let's move on to creditor three; those glorious credit cards.

* * * * *

Chapter 11
"Those Amazing Credit Cards"

Here's my definition of a credit card: "It's a process for using tomorrow's money, for what you bought yesterday, to pay for today's enjoyment – that could cost you a life-time."

To gauge the power of credit card companies; I decided to see how many credit card offers I would receive in one year. I'm not sure these pictures grasp the magnitude; however, I stopped saving credit card offers when the total reached 250.

> ▸ **Yes, I received 250 credit card solicitations in less than one year.**

Now, think about this. Let's say that all those (unopened by the way) credit cards offered at least a $10,000 line of credit.

That would total $2,500,000. **I now had two-million five hundred thousand in credit card open-to-buy money.**

I got credit card offers from every company and store you can imagine; gas cards, department stores, insurance companies, airlines, hotels, I mean you name it, and I received it.

Look at this stack of credit card offers bundled in stacks of 50! Two hundred and fifty card offers! That's just crazy!

So, why do you think these credit card companies keep sending me card after card after card?

Let's explore!

Ever wonder why you see all those commercials on TV offering you all those credit cards? Ever wonder why you get all those little envelopes in the mail offering you a brand new credit card? If your mailman is like mine, he brings you several credit card offers every month.

Why is that? Why did I receive so many credit card offers?

I imagine those credit card company executives were sitting in their big expensive offices saying, "This Nathan guy is not giving us any of his money, and we want it. So, let's keep sending him more credit card offers!" Actually, this may be closer to the truth than we may know.

And here's another question I have.

What do they really mean when they say; "What's in your wallet?"

Well, here might be part of the answer:

▸ The "average credit card debt among households with balances on their credit cards is $16,048."
— Federal Reserve

I think it is obvious why they ask; "What's in your wallet?" Do you suppose it is, so they too, can own part, if not all, of your $16,048?

I don't think they are really asking a question at all. I think they are making a statement of, "We WANT what's in your wallet!"

What do you say?

The answer is very simple; creditors want all your money.

Not only does the mortgage company want all your money, the automobile company wants all your money, and the credit card companies, likewise, wants all your money.

And, guess what? They will take it as long as you are willing to give it to them!

Creditors are in the business to make money – **Your** **Money!**

How serious are the credit card challenges people face today?

Well, here are a few statistics that should cause people to re-think their credit card usage:

- ▶ Consumers have on average a total of 9 credit cards — myFico.com

- ▶ 6 billion credit card offers are mailed annually — Synovate

- ▶ Total balances due on credit cards today stands at nearly $762 billion — U.S. Federal Reserve

- ▶ $90 billion in fees are paid annually to the credit card industry — CreditCards.com

Consumers with an average of 9 credit cards racking up $762 billion on them; and, paying $90 billion in fees.

Don't you think there is better use for your money?

Unfortunately, most people only look at two numbers when determining if they will buy on credit.

Ill-advisedly they fall into the Monthly Payment Trap!

People buy in terms of monthly payments. Regrettably, they do not look at the long-term total cost of the items:

- ▶ People Consider Two Numbers:
    1) Their monthly income, and
    2) Their total monthly expenses
- ▶ If a new "Monthly Payment" fits in their "Monthly Income" ...THEY BUY

Many people don't realize how much interest they pay to their credit card company, because the payments are in small increments over a long period of time. For example, let's say you have an outstanding balance of $2,000 for new furniture and your interest rate is 18%.

Making the minimum 2% or $10 payment, the interest cost over the loan period would be $4,807. Oh yes, the payoff period; over 30 years. How will the furniture look in 30 years?

Your minimum payment of only 2% or $10 sounds really good, doesn't it? However, if you just pay the minimum payment, your $2,000 furniture in reality cost you $6,807.

Now how many of us would have bought if the salesperson had said that our real cost would be $6,807? Well, the answer is quite simple.

- ▶ **Not one of us would make such a choice!**

However, that is why you are here today; to learn how to avoid these types of traps. And, once you're armed with this knowledge, you also can, come from a position of strength.

Credit card companies love people who run up big charge amounts and keep high balances on their cards. Why?

Because they love collecting 18% to 25%, or more, interest from you.

> ▸ **I'm telling you, they will take every dollar you will give to them!**

And what happens if you get behind or late with payments?

Well, in addition to the 18% to 25% interest, they love charging you big fees for being late on your payments, they love charging you big fees for being over your credit limit, they love charging you big cash advance fees, and most of all they love YOU for giving them ALL YOUR MONEY.

And, with the typical family having credit card balances of $16,048 the credit card industry's solution to their situation is to offer more credit cards. I once saw an ad on TV where a particular credit card company said they have 900 different credit cards "for your convenience." In other words, they have 900 ways of taking every penny you have!

> ▸ *"Those who understand compound interest are destined to collect it. Those who don't are doomed to pay it."* ...Albert Einstein

If credit card companies can get you hooked, they will own you for all of your financial life. This is why our youth get bombarded with credit card offers at such a young age. They want to "collect from them" their entire life!

Oh, and when you are out of money, don't worry, because I'm sure they will be right there to take care of all your needs. And yes, I'm being extremely sarcastic. It's just like your mortgage company. Think you actually own your home? Miss three or four payments, and see who really owns your home. Sadly, too many people are learning this harsh reality.

And before we wrap up this topic, let me add an industry that is crushing the young people of today – Student Loans!

According to the Federal Reserve Bank, outstanding student loan debt is between 902 Billion and **1.3 Trillion** dollars. The average Class of 2017 graduate has $38,000 in student loan debt. And, for the borrower aged 20 to 30, the average monthly student loan payment is approximately $351.00.

Student loan debt has overtaken the total amount of credit card debt. At the time of this writing, outstanding credit card debt is approximately $762 billion.

Our graduates are faced with mounting financial challenges when carrying this type of debt. How long would it take someone making, for example, $40,000 per year, to pay back an estimated $38,000 in just student loan debt? The years to recover could be a life time.

Let me add this about the impacts of debt. There is way more than financial cost to carrying high balances of debt.

There are emotional costs of anxiety, stress and strained relationships. Plus, people are faced with the potential for physical hardships on their body of having a lack of sleep, being tired on the job, and the impacts of weight issues.

It's not just about the money. It's potentially about your overall health and family relationships.

There are other reasons why you must keep your debt in check and work to become debt free.

Let me share another personal story of how being debt free impacted our two daughters. When it was time for them to go off to college, my wife and I were committed to them so they would not come out of college with student loans.

Over the years we had saved money for their college. What we faced during that time, unexpectedly, was not only one daughter attending an in-state college, our other daughter attended an out-of-state college; and when she crossed state lines; the tuition went through the roof.

However, at the same time they were in school, my wife was also in college finishing her master's degree as a teacher. Three in college at the same time!   Sound familiar?

What was the benefit of my family being debt free when my two daughters, and wife, were all in college? In addition to what we had saved, plus my daughter's scholarship money, we were able to pay cash for what was a total of 10 years, collectively; for the time the three of them were in school.

That's the benefit of being debt free.

You see, jobs and income can stop, but the bills, and debt payments, they will keep on coming.

Hey, give your creditors all the rest of your 2.2 million dollars, and guess what, they will take it. Don't let this happen to you. Live Debt Free – put your money to work for you!

And people wonder why 95% of people retire flat broke!

It's time to stop this madness! It's time to take control of your financial life! It's time to think differently! I have great passion about the message we are bringing to you today.

I've seen the impact debt has on people. I've known people who've made big money and were broke. I've known people who made significantly less money and were in total financial control. I've seen, time after time after time, it's a question of debt levels, not income, which keeps a family down.

This is very serious business and I want you in control of your financial life. I have more concepts to discuss regarding how money works and how you can take action!

You can begin to turn the tables on your creditors. You can keep more of your money. You can start on your road to becoming totally debt free, including owning your home. You can pay cash for everything.

You can start building real wealth.

And, then, you will have more ownership of your time!

corund©123RF.com

* * * * *

Chapter 12
"Rule of 72 – The Most Powerful Rule In Finance"

Concept 3 – Present and Future Value of Money

I had to learn how to appreciate the value and limitations of money. Or, I should say, view them differently. It was part of my paradigm shift.

You can become wealthy by understanding the principles of consistency, the time value of money, and the Rule of 72.

▶ What is the time value of money?

▶ How can time and compound interest build financial independence?

▶ Why is it important to understand the Rule of 72?

And, how can being out of debt, allow you to then use those same dollars now paying for debt, to build your wealth?

Understand the most powerful rule in finance: the Rule of 72:

The Rule of 72 states: to find the approximate number of years it takes for your money to double, divide the interest rate of return into 72.

For example: how often does a one-time deposit of $10,000 double in value?

▶ At 3% return – it takes 24 years for your money to double from $10,000 to $20,000 (72 / 3% = 24 years)

▶ At 6% return – it takes 12 years for your money to double from $10,000 to $20,000 (72 / 6% = 12 years).

- At 12% return – it takes 6 years for your money to double from $10,000 to $20,000 (72 / 12% = 6 years).

The chart below shows the series of your money doubling based on the interest rate earned through a total of 48 years.

Number of Years	3%	6%	12%
0	$10,000	$10,000	$10,000
6			$20,000
12		$20,000	$40,000
18			$80,000
24	$20,000	$40,000	$160,000
30			$320,000
36		$80,000	$640,000
42			$1,280,000
48	$40,000	$160,000	$2,560,000

It is important to understand that every additional percentage of return you make on your money can literally mean thousands of dollars to you.

In 48 years at 3% the initial $10,000 has now grown to $40,000. However, by doubling your return from 3% to 6%, you have $160,000. Your interest rate only doubled (from 3% to 6%); however, your money quadrupled from $40,000 to $160,000.

And look at what happens to your money total when the interest rate of return doubles from 6% to 12%. Again, even though the interest rate doubles, your money total, well let's just say, it goes through the roof!

The mortgage companies, the banks and the credit card industry more than comprehend the power of the Rule of 72. Banks give you a very small rate of return for you to "save" your money in their bank.

And the credit card industry, well, they charge anywhere from 18% - 25% (or more) for you to use their money.

How much do you think the credit card industry makes each year by charging you 18% - 25%?

Look at it this way. How often will your money double sitting in the "bank savings account" from the big 1% banks give to you? (Yep, 72 years).

Now, how often will money double for the credit card industry at 18%?

Who would you like this Rule of 72 working for?

‣ Your bank

‣ Your credit union

‣ Your car loan company

‣ Your mortgage company

‣ Your credit card company, or

‣ **YOU**

Here's another simple question about the value of $1.00:

What is the real power and worth of $1.00? What truly happens to the value of $1.00 by understanding the time value of money?

Can you systematically turn one dollar per day into $105,428?

The answer – YES! Most definitely!

By saving $1 a day, $30 per month, or $360 per year, and receiving an 8% return, in 40 years it will grow to $105,428.

And, when you chart it out, you can see how your money grows over time to a total of $105,428.

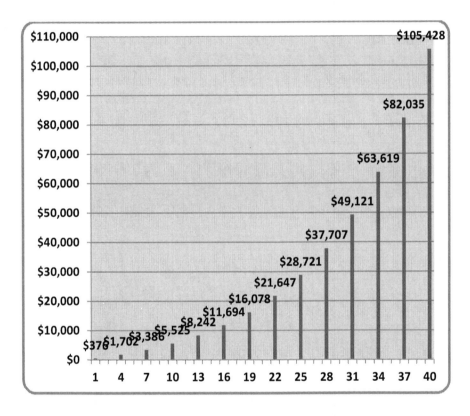

In this example, over the 40 years, you saved a total of $14,400 ($360 x 40 years). However, the time value of money and the compound interest factor have grown your money to a total of $105,428.

That is total interest generated (in your pocket) of $91,028.

Think about the huge impact to your savings. You deposited $14,400, have an additional $91,028 in interest, to now total $105,428 in your bank account.

Now, I understand that utilizing this example really serves to illustrate the "power" and "potential" for understanding the time value of money concept. Saving $1.00 per day is not a stretch of the imagination.

However, my real goal is to start you thinking. My goal is to create a thought process that allows you to see the impact of how just $1.00 per day can add up to significant dollars over a period of time.

By illustrating this concept with smaller dollar examples, that when we apply larger numbers to the savings factor, you will understand exactly what will happen to your bank account and total savings!

You see, on one hand, you truly don't have to make a lot of money to become financially independent. You just have to know, understand, and then put into practice these simple concepts.

Then, as you start to apply the concepts illustrated throughout this book, it is like powerful forces hitting at the same time to create the "perfect storm" in your financial position. It has the power to change your financial future.

Okay, so we understand the power and potential of saving just $1.00 per day.

Now, what happens to the totals if you save $5.00 a day?

Do you know that by saving $5.00 a day, getting 8% interest, that in 40 years it will grow to $527,142?

You are saving only $150 a month. That is a savings over the 40 years of $72,000.

And the total interest generated and paid to you...? $455,142

Now we are starting to talk about more serious money!

And, when you chart it out, you can see how your money grows over time.

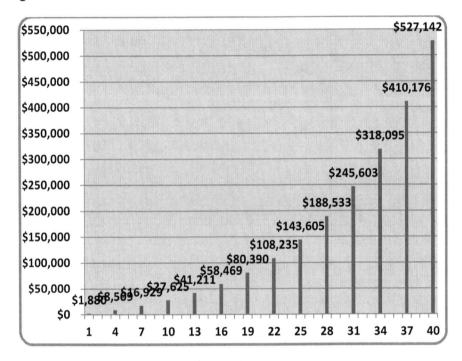

And, what if you eliminated $2,000 a month in debt and then turned those dollars into wealth generating income?

Just imagine how your financial life would be if you eliminated all your monthly debt payments and then had those same dollars to live on and to generate savings for you!

You see, as previously stated, you don't necessarily have to make a lot of money to become financially independent.

You have to know, understand, and then put into practice these, what can be, life-changing concepts.

Here's the point of using the $1.00 example to illustrate how your money is working for you. It helps to clarify and to understand the value of every dollar you earn.

Let's say you buy something for $1.00 and pay $1.00 cash for it. Okay, that's good. But, let's say, you buy something for $1.00, finance it, and then end up paying $5.00 for it. This is where debt will put the squeeze on you.

▸ **Don't let it.**

You can make a difference for yourself and for your family. It takes a commitment, it takes some personal discipline, it takes being consistent on your plan, and it takes persistence.

Put your debt elimination plan into action; experience the benefits of living debt free, be content, and decide what kind of difference you want to make.

Let me give you another example of how time and compound interest can work for you.

* * * * *

"What you do makes a difference; and you have to decide what kind of difference you want to make." ... Jane Goodall

Chapter 13
"How To Get Your Money To Work Hard For You"

Let's say that at age 19 you invest $2,000 a year into your mutual fund and you do so from ages 19 to 26 getting a 10% rate of return. For 8 years you put in your $2,000 and then stop; not putting in any more money in the coming years.

At this point your total contribution into your mutual fund is $16,000.

Now let's say that your friend waits 8 years to begin investing. And now at age 27 starts investing $2,000 per year. And, let's say that your friend contributes $2,000 per year until reaching the age of 65.

That would be 39 years and a total of $78,000.

Now here is my question for you. At age 65, who has more money? You, after starting at age 19 and only investing $16,000 over just 8 years, or your friend who waited 8 years before starting at age 27 and invested $78,000 over 39 years?

▸ **The answer may surprise you.**

At age 65, you would have a total of $1,035,121 and your friend would have a total of $883,185.

Imagine that; you invested only $16,000, your friend $78,000 and you have over $150,000 more! Plus, your friend invested $62,000 more into their account than you.

As stated, you don't have to make a boat load of money to become financially independent. **Knowledge is Power.** And with this knowledge you can utilize and leverage the power of time and compound interest. It can make you more secure.

The following illustrates this comparison example.

$2,000 Savings Per Year - 10% Interest

Results Summary	
Starting amount	$0
Years	8 & 39
Additional contributions	$2,000 per year
Rate of return	10.00% compounded annually
Total amount you will have invested	$16,000 & $78,000
Total at end of investment	$1,035,121 & $883,185

Savings Balance by Year

Age	Total Investments	Ending Balance	Total Investments	Ending Balance
19	$2,000	$2,200		
20	$2,000	$4,620		
21	$2,000	$7,282		
22	$2,000	$10,210		
23	$2,000	$13,431		
24	$2,000	$16,974		
25	$2,000	$20,872		
26	$2,000	$25,158		
27		$27,673	$2,000	$2,200
28		$30,441	$2,000	$4,620
29		$33,485	$2,000	$7,282
30		$36,833	$2,000	$10,210
31		$40,517	$2,000	$13,431
32		$44,568	$2,000	$16,974
33		$49,025	$2,000	$20,872
34		$53,928	$2,000	$25,158
35		$59,321	$2,000	$29,874
36		$65,253	$2,000	$35,062
37		$71,778	$2,000	$40,768
38		$78,956	$2,000	$47,045
39		$86,852	$2,000	$53,949

Age	Total Investments	Ending Balance	Total Investments	Ending Balance
40		$95,537	$2,000	$61,544
41		$105,091	$2,000	$69,899
42		$115,600	$2,000	$79,089
43		$127,160	$2,000	$89,198
44		$139,876	$2,000	$100,318
45		$153,864	$2,000	$112,550
46		$169,250	$2,000	$126,005
47		$186,175	$2,000	$140,805
48		$204,793	$2,000	$157,086
49		$225,272	$2,000	$174,994
50		$247,799	$2,000	$194,694
51		$272,579	$2,000	$216,363
52		$299,837	$2,000	$240,199
53		$329,821	$2,000	$266,419
54		$362,803	$2,000	$295,261
55		$399,083	$2,000	$326,988
56		$438,992	$2,000	$361,886
57		$482,891	$2,000	$400,275
58		$531,180	$2,000	$442,503
59		$584,298	$2,000	$488,953
60		$642,728	$2,000	$540,048
61		$707,001	$2,000	$596,253
62		$777,701	$2,000	$658,079
63		$855,471	$2,000	$726,086
64		$941,019	$2,000	$800,895
65		$1,035,121	$2,000	$883,185
Totals	$16,000		$78,000	

This is an example of how compound interest can work for you. This is how "time" can work for you. This is why you must get out of debt as soon as possible, why you must not let creditors take every penny you make, and why you must get your money to start working for you.

If you don't start now, when will you start? And if you wait, will you ever start? And if you wait, will you end up as one of the 95% who never make it financially? There is only one person that can make those choices for you.

▸ **And that one person is you!**

It pays to start now. When you don't, there's a high cost to waiting. The chart below shows savings of $100 per month and earning 9% interest for 40 years.

When you start now, in 40 years, you will have $471,640.

However, by waiting just one year to start your savings, (at $100 per month that is $1,200 you did not invest), it costs you $41,600.

You can see the negative impact of waiting one year! It's significant. And look what happens if you wait 5 years or 15 years to start saving.

Wait 5 years, and in this example, your money grows to $296,380, and it costs you $175,260 in total savings.

You simply can't wait to get started on your debt elimination and wealth building plan! It can cost you a lot of money.

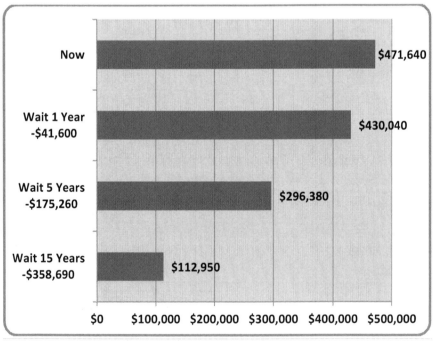

Here is another disaster waiting to happen:

> ▸ "44% of Americans said they simply *guessed* what they would need (to save) for a comfortable retirement"
> — US News and World Report online

Don't be one of those who simply guess at what you need for retirement. You must start now! It does not matter what age you are now (younger or older) the decision you must make is to start – and to start now!

There is a saying, "If it is to be, it's up to me." You must recognize that all the mortgage companies, credit card companies, and creditors really care about is how much of your money they can take from you over your working life. Once you realize this, you must accept that what happens is really up to you and you can be in control.

And if you are not in command of your situation, don't have your debts under control, and something outside of your power goes haywire in your universe, then what will you do?

▸ **Let me explain what I once experienced.**

I didn't always have that middle of the road retail job. Over the years I worked my way up the corporate ladder (after I became debt free) and eventually joined a large, well-known financial services company as a senior manager of operations. I had approximately 200 people in my line of responsibility.

As time passed, the company made a corporate decision to change their business model. What does that mean? Well, it means they started moving their operational jobs overseas. It's called outsourcing. You may be way too familiar with that term. It was only a question of time before my job and the jobs of many business associates would be shipped overseas and be eliminated and gone forever.

Those next few months were very painful. I had people asking me, "Nathan, do you think my job will be eliminated?" Or, "What will I do? I can't afford to lose my job." I could see fear in their eyes as many of them had recently purchased a larger home or were first time home owners, had small babies at home, or were close to retirement age, and I would venture to say, most had probably committed their earnings to their creditors.

There was panic and fear from many of my co-workers wondering how they would pay their creditors and survive financially. Many were beyond just being scared.

They were terrified!

> ▸ **And while my heart felt for them, it was at this time that I really understood the importance of what it means to be totally debt free.**

You see, as I define it for myself, you don't have to be rich to be financially independent. Financially independent meant for me that after leaving work for the day, while we still had work, I drove my "paid for car" to my "paid for house" and in my hip pocket I had a "zero balance" on the one credit card I kept for emergencies.

I did not have to worry about keeping a roof over my family's head or food on the table. **This is the power that being in control of your financial position can give to you.**

It took several months but eventually the day came and we got the pink slip that our positions were eliminated due to outsourcing. Thousands of people walked out the corporate door for the very last time that day; me included.

Thousands of people realized a painful truth that day. And that is, we cannot allow our financial future to be left up to a job, the government, luck, chance, or social security. The end result rests with us and the knowledge we must acquire.

Our future depends on the decisions we make regarding how we protect our earnings and our earning power.

> ▸ **As Abraham Lincoln said, "Always bear in mind that your own resolution to succeed is more important than any other thing."**

In this book you can gain the knowledge needed to succeed.

You see the answer is not always in having to make a lot of money to achieve financial independence, it is not in working a second or third job to make ends meet, it's about using your money wisely and in knowing how to get it to work for you.

It's understanding how powerful $1.00 can be to you.

It's about knowledge. Knowledge of how money really works, knowledge of how to get out of debt, and knowledge of how to use compound interest to change your financial direction; to live debt free. This is what I mean by working hard for your money and having your money work hard for you!

Let's go back to the example of your home being paid off in 15 years. We reviewed this process previously on page 58. To review, we had paid off $470 of debt, added that to our $1,330 mortgage payment, for a total of $1,800 being paid on the mortgage. The result: mortgage is paid off in 15 years!

Recap – Mortgage Payoff - $470 Fast Track:

> ▸ $470 Per Month: Additional Principal Payment
> ▸ Reduce Mortgage: 15 Years and 0 Months
> ▸ Total Savings: $155,847

Now, instead of paying money to the mortgage company, you invest it – for yourself!

Think about what you've accomplished. You have paid off your home; so now, let's take the regular mortgage payment of $1,330 plus the $470 of eliminated debt, and continue "paying" it out. **Let's put that $1,800 to work for you!**

You are going to "pay" the $1,800 to yourself and put it into, for example, a mutual fund, annuity, or other investment. This is getting your money to work for you!

Continue this for the next 15 years, **the same time period that you would have been paying your mortgage,** earn a 6½% return, and in 15 years **you will have $549,340.**

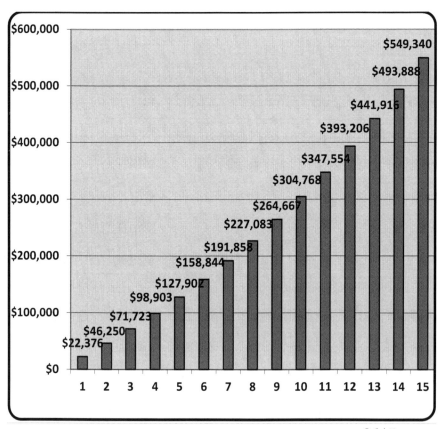

Remember, this is all your money.

The question is, are you going to keep it and build financial independence or let the creditors have it all? Well, we now know the answer to that question, don't we?

Consider this scenario:

You pay off your home in 15 years. It's now free and clear.

Your friend however, continues to make his regular monthly house payment for 30 years.

After that 30 year period, your friend has:
  1) A house that is paid for, and
  2) Basically no money in the bank

You on the other hand have:
  1) A house that is paid for, and
  2) $549,340 in the bank

Which financial path would you prefer to take? Are you willing to make some changes? Are you willing to make the necessary changes today, to have a better tomorrow?

▶ **You can get your money to work for you. It works. You can do it!**

* * * * *

"I used to say, "I sure hope things will change." Then I learned that the only way things are going to change for me is when I change." ... Jim Rohn

Chapter 14
"Never Make Another Debt Or Mortgage Payment Again"

Concept 4 – How to Systematically Eliminate All Your Debts

72soul©123RF.com

Some people think the problem is not making enough money. You may also think the only way to get out of debt or to have more spendable money is to make more money.

However, the solution to the problem is not in always making more money. The real problem, for most people, is in accumulating too much debt.

Would you like to have money to do the things you like? How about money to help your family? Take a vacation? Give to your church? How about money to support your former school? How about money to support a charity or give to those less fortunate?

How about having enough money to tell your boss "goodbye?"

The solution is not in always making more money. It is in spending less, getting out of debt, and then using your money to work for you. You have to stop the flow of your money to creditors and start the flow into your pockets.

Want to have an extra, say, $400 per month? Would you like to do that by not having to get a permanent part-time job?

Note: There are times when you have to do what you have to do. So, a part-time job can help eliminate those debts faster. I had a client who, after working all day, delivered pizzas on the weekends so he could get out of debt. And... he did get out of debt! Then, he stopped delivering pizzas.

> ▸ **Live like you've never lived before...**
> **So you can live like you've never lived before!**

You can have $400 per month by eliminating $400 of debts.

Think about this, how much does that pizza every weekend really cost you, $25 per week or about $100 a month? How much does that fast food lunch cost you every day, $10 a day or about $200 a month?

How much does that hot cup of latte coffee cost you every morning on your way to work, about $6.00 a day or about $100 a month?

Well, add all those up, plus look for other areas and items you can reduce spending, and I say that $400 could be your start to eliminating all your debts. That $400 could be working for you to build your financial independence.

Now I'm not saying that you can't indulge in things you like. Nor is this about keeping a journal of every penny you spend. You don't have to struggle, deprive yourself, or stress out.

I'm just saying that if you review where all your money is going now, you can still indulge, just a little less. Then you will have significant dollars to use for eliminating debts.

> ▸ **Okay, so let's talk about how to eliminate all your debts using the Debt Stacking Plan.**

I can teach you how to do this in about 5 minutes.

That may sound too simplistic to believe. However, I'm going to share a little secret with you. I can teach you how to become debt free, how to build wealth, and how you can achieve financial independence. And, yes, I can teach you in about 5 minutes.

Now, there is a hard part to all of this. (And, let me say, this may be the most important line you read in this entire book.)

> ▸ **The hard part: Making the commitment to do it!**

To make some sacrifices today, so that you can put your money to work for you, so that one day your money will be doing all the work for you. Making that decision and doing it is the hard part.

> ▸ **"It's in your moments of decision that your destiny is shaped."** ... Anthony Robbins

My moment of decision? The day that shaped my destiny?

> ▸ **July 25, 1996**

This was the exact day I made the decision to change my financial future. That's the day the "commitment" was made.

I knew on that day that I had to change my thought process regarding how to handle money and my creditors.

I knew that if things were going to change for my family that I had to make some changes. The "commitment" made to my wife, my children and to myself was unwavering. Nothing was going to alter my path to becoming debt free. NOTHING!

July 25, 1996... I knew on that day...

- ▶ It Was Time To Think Differently...
- ▶ It Was Time To Take A New Path...
- ▶ It Was Time For A Paradigm Shift!

The following "transformation" shows it quite clearly about the change made on that July day.

I knew I did not want to be under the stress of debt anymore. I knew I did not want creditors to control me. I wanted to live again – dream again – take more control of my life again.

So, on July 25, 1996, I "changed just like that"...

teptong©123RF.com

Is today, the moment of decision for you! Is today, the day, which will shape your financial future? Your financial destiny?

Is today, the day, you make the decision to start on your road to financial independence; to live debt free?

Is today, the day, you "Change just like that?"

Do you want a life of financial well-being? To live debt free?

Do you want to be able to buy income-producing assets that will provide a residual interest income for you?

You have to be the protector of your wealth. As I have repeated many times, the credit card companies, mortgage companies, and other creditors want all your money.

The question is, are you willing to do what it takes so that **YOU** will be in the 5% group that is financially independent?

So, what is the game plan for getting out of debt? Are you ready to see how to do it?

▶ **The very first rule for getting out of debt is to not generate any new debts.**

My advice – cut up all but one of your credit cards. Or, do like my friend did, and freeze all of them in the refrigerator!

You have to get your credit cards and debt under control. Do not create any additional or new debt on top of what you already owe to your creditors.

* * * * *

"Your present circumstances don't determine where you can go; they merely determine where you start." ... Nido Qubein

Chapter 15
"Your Debt Stacking Plan – The Process"

Okay, here we go! As my oldest daughter would say, "Let's do this!" How to get out of debt? This may be your most important 5 minutes.

Make a list of all your debts. Not your bills but your debts. Bills are expenses like the electric bill or the water bill. Bills come every month and you can never pay them off. Debts are amounts you owe, that you can totally pay off.

First, make a list of all your debts.

On your list, put down your car amount(s), your credit card amount(s), your retail store credit card amount(s), your gas card(s), and your mortgage amount. Add to the list any and all debts that you can totally pay off.

Second, arrange your debts by outstanding balance.

Put as number one the debt with the smallest balance and put as number two the debt with the next higher balance, and so on until you have arranged all your debts from the smallest to the largest balance. And, in most all cases, your mortgage will be the one with the largest balance and will be listed last.

Let's discuss how to eliminate all your debts and in what order to pay them off.

> ▸ **The plan is to create a laser focus to eliminate all your debts as quickly as possible.**

Third, starting with debt number <u>two</u> and going through to what is probably your highest balance, your mortgage, you will make only the minimum payment each month.

On debt number <u>one</u>, you are going to pay the minimum payment, plus a portion of your extra money. The extra money is coming from spending less on pizza, spending less on the fast food lunches, and spending less on areas over which you have to take control.

You have to look for areas in your spending that are like waters flowing out of a hole in a dam. You have to make important decisions about how you want your financial future to look. Spend it all now and always have someone else in control of your time. Or, position your money to work hard for you, so that you are in control of your financial future!

Even if you can only start with an extra payment of $25 to $100 per month to reduce your debts, it will be the beginning of you becoming totally debt free and owning both your time and your freedom. Start with whatever amount you can.

We are going to call this extra money your **Freedom Fund.**

Okay, so here is how you are going to focus your debt elimination plan to pay off all your debts.

On debt number one, pay <u>both</u> the minimum amount <u>plus</u> your Freedom Fund amount. Let's say for example, that on your smallest debt, you owe $375. The minimum payment is $25, and you have $100 in your Freedom Fund. That means you are now paying $125 per month on debt number one.

Look what will happen. In only 3 months you will have this debt paid off. **One debt down!**

Okay, now on to debt number two which is $700. How much do you have to apply to debt two? Well, you have the minimum payment, <u>plus</u> your $100 Freedom Fund, <u>plus</u> the $25 that was the minimum payment from debt one.

So, let's say that the minimum payment on debt number two is $50. Add them up, and you realize that you have $50 from debt two, $25 from debt number one, plus your $100 Freedom Fund for a total of $175.

With a balance on debt two of $700, by making the payment of $175 each month, you will have debt number two totally paid off in 4 months. Remember, on all your other debts, you continue making only the minimum monthly payments.

Now to debt number three. You owe $825 on debt three and the minimum payment is $100. At this point I hope you realize that you are gaining momentum on wiping out all your debts and doing it with a systematic and effective approach.

If you add payments of $25 from debt one, $50 from debt two, $100 from debt three, plus your $100 Freedom Fund, you now have a total of $275 to pay every month against debt number three. You owe $825 on debt number three. Do the math and you see that you will have debt number three eliminated in just 3 months. **Two more debts down!**

On to debt number four of which you owe $7,425. The minimum payment is $400. Your prior minimum debt payments totaled $175, plus the $100 Freedom Fund, plus this $400 minimum, for a total of $675. Making this payment, debt four will totally be paid off in 11 months!

▸ **Let's recap what has happened with these 4 debts. In just 21 months, you have eliminated $9,325 and freed up $675 in monthly cash flow.**

Now, your actual amounts will vary and your Freedom Fund may be more or it may be less than $100. The process works.

The key is to start eliminating your debts and to eliminate them with this systematic approach. Follow the process!

Does this Debt Stacking Plan work?

▸ **Yes it works.**

▸ **This is exactly the plan I followed which got me out of debt in just over six years.**

The following Debt Stacking Strategy outlines the example.

Debt Payoff Strategy
Example

PROCESS STEPS:

1. List all debts from the smallest to the largest balance.

2. Make the minimum payments on all debts except # 1.

3. On # 1, make the minimum, plus your Freedom Fund.

4. When debt # 1 is paid off, add what was that minimum payment amount to your Freedom Fund. This will be your new Freedom Fund total for debt # 2.

   As you continue to pay off a debt, add what was that minimum payment to your Freedom Fund.

5. Put the type of debt in column "A"

6. Put the balance of the debt in column "B"

7. Put the minimum monthly payment in column "C"

8. Put in your Freedom Fund amount in column "D"

9. Put your total payment (C + D) in column "E"

10. Calculate the number of months (B ÷ E) to pay off the debt in "F"

Column A	Column B	Column C	Column D	Column E	Column F
Debt Type	Outstanding Balance	Minimum Payment	Freedom Fund	Total Payment	Payoff Months
Debt # 1	$375	$25	$100	$125	3
Debt # 2	$700	$50	$125	$175	4
Debt # 3	$825	$100	$175	$275	3
Debt # 4	$7,425	$400	$275	$675	11
Debt # 5	$100,500	$1,000	$675	$1,675	60
				Months To Become Debt Free	81
				Years To Become Debt Free	6 Years 9 Months

Debt free, in this example, in 81 months: 6 years / 9 months. Does the process work? **YES!** Worth going through? **YES!**

As you apply these concepts on a consistent and persistent basis, the other thing that starts happening is that you start feeling less pressure as your debts begin disappearing.

You are starting to see light at the end of the tunnel.

It is the start of your new beginning! Simply continue this process until every debt you have is paid off.

Continue rolling the minimum monthly payments into the next debt and look for additional monies to add to your Freedom Fund. Your only variable then to being debt free is time.

* * * *

Chapter 16
"Build Your Freedom Fund"

And, speaking of additional money let me share two additional potential sources with you, as we've already talked about a part-time job, to increase the amount of your Freedom Fund;

1) Tax withholdings, and

2) A home-based business!

Are you giving the federal government an interest free loan?

Another potential source of money for your Freedom Fund is to review your tax withholdings. The average tax refund is approximately $3,120. That is an over payment each month of $260. By adjusting your tax withholdings to increase take-home pay, this could seriously add to your Freedom Fund.

You are letting the government use your money without paying you any interest. How can you leverage this "interest free loan" for yourself?

Well, instead of letting your money sit (interest free with the government) year after year – either invest that money each month, or add it to your Freedom Fund to pay off your debts.

What is the financial benefit to you?

The following chart shows how your money will grow based on investing $260 every month (the monthly tax withholding overpayment amount), for 35 years, and at various interest rate of return. Even if you just put the $260 each month for 35 years into a cookie jar you would still have $109,200.

Review your tax withholdings and make any adjustments carefully so that you do not owe at the end of the year.

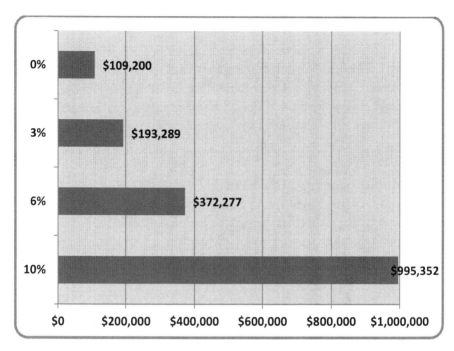

0%	$109,200				
3%	$193,289				
6%		$372,277			
10%					$995,352

$0 $200,000 $400,000 $600,000 $800,000 $1,000,000

This money can be a great source to jump start your Freedom Fund to more aggressively payoff your debts!

Next; an additional source of money to consider building your Freedom Fund, is with your own home-based business.

A home-based business gives you the flexibility of working from the comfort of your own home. It enables you to work your business as your time and schedule permit. This benefit also allows you to have more family time!

Also, there are tax benefits to having your own home-based business that a part-time job usually does not provide. In most cases, with a home-based business you can take various tax deductions for business expenses.

A home-based business may be a consideration for you to increase your Freedom Fund.

* * * * *

Chapter 17
"Your Final Mortgage Payment"

Okay, back to your Debt Stacking Plan. After you have eliminated these initial debts, it is now time to focus all your payments on eliminating debt number five. This last debt is usually your home mortgage.

Yes, you are now ready to pay off your home so that you own it free and clear. At this point you have $675 in your total Freedom Fund. This is the total of all the other minimum payments, plus your original Freedom Fund amount.

As an example, let's say you owe $100,500 on debt five, and the payment is $1,000. Add this to your Freedom Fund and you have $1,675 to pay on this last debt every month. Again, this last debt will usually be your mortgage payment. Under this example, you would pay off debt five in only 60 months.

In just five years, you have eliminated this last debt 100%.

Consider what has occurred in this example.

▸ **You have eliminated $109,825 of debts, and in only 6 years and 9 months you are totally debt free. You now own everything free and clear, all your debts are gone, and you can use those debt payment dollars to start building real wealth.**

This is your Debt Stacking Plan.

Numbers on the following chart, though not totally exact because of overall interest; are however, directionally correct. By taking the Freedom Fund of $100 adding it to your minimum payment, you can systematically pay off your debts.

What I want you to understand is the concept. It works!

The Debt Stacking Plan * Freedom Fund = $100

	Debt Amount	Minimum Payment	* Plus $100			
Debt 1	$375	$25	$125			
			↓			
Debt 2	$700	$50	($50 + $125)	$175		
				↓		
Debt 3	$825	$100		($100 + $175)	$275	
					↓	
Debt 4	$7,425	$400			($400 + $275)	$675
						↓
Debt 5	$100,500	$1,000				$1,675
Total	$109,825	$1,575	$1,675			

Debt # 1: Paid Off 3 Months   ($375 / $125)
Debt # 2: Paid Off 4 Months   ($700 / $175)
Debt # 3: Paid Off 3 Months   ($825 / $275)
Debt # 4: Paid Off 11 Months   ($7,425 / $675)
Debt # 5: Paid Off 60 Months   ($100,500 / $1,675)
Debt Freedom Date: 81 months = 6 years & 9 months

Time passes! This we know to be true. You and I will be somewhere in 6 years and 9 months. The question is, where?

My question is, are you willing to do these things that will make you totally debt free during this time? Or, will you find yourself further down life's road only to be in the same financial situation as you are today?

Think about this next step on your road to achieving financial independence.

Let's assume you followed this process and paid everything off in 10 years; including your mortgage. You can now put a minimum of $1,675 into an investment program. And based on what was a 30 year mortgage, you can make this $1,675 deposit per month for the next 20 years.

This 20 year period is the same amount of time that you would normally have been paying for your house.

▸ **Want to be a millionaire with cash in the bank?**

At $1,675 per month, for 20 years, earning an 8½% return; you will accumulate $1,057,662. You are on track to becoming a millionaire! See below how your money grows.

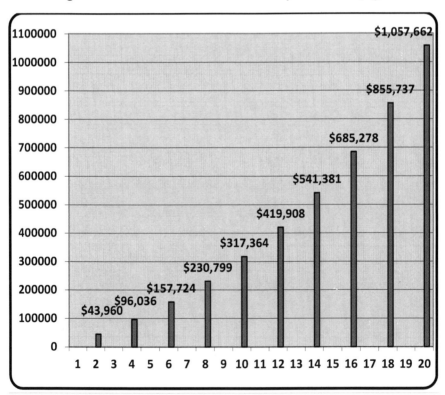

Now what happens?

Your car is paid for, you have no credit card debts, all your other debts are paid off, and your home is also 100% paid for free and clear!

You are saving money and starting to have your money work for you. Stress level is way down. Worrying about how to make ends meet is way down.

- ▸ **You are now significantly less impacted if the economy takes a turn for the worse.**

- ▸ **You are now significantly less impacted if your company can only give a small raise this year.**

- ▸ **You are now significantly less impacted if the company you work for outsources your job and sends it overseas.**

Starting to see the picture?

You are now more significantly in control of your financial life.

You are now in control... period!

It took me just over 6 years to complete this process and become 100% debt free. You too can become 100% debt free. You can accomplish this and do it in a reasonable period of time.

I trust at this time, you can understand why our mission is to help you: *"Live Debt Free."*

And, just a side thought, I have had people ask me over the years about those who make a lot of money. Isn't it easier for them to pay off their debts? Can't they do it faster?

No, not really. Most people have debt levels relative to their income levels. Make more money, have more debts. Make less money, have less debts. It's all relative.

When I started my debt elimination plan, my total debt balance was more than double from what is used in the Debt Stacking example. However, even on my modest retail job income, and my wife's teacher salary, we became debt free in just over 6 years.

Your debts may be more or they may be less than the examples used to explain this process. The current interest rates, compared to the examples used, may now be more or they may now be less. However, the key is to understand the process. The goal is to start the process of eliminating all your debts.

▶ **Start Today!**

Once you start to see your debts going away, once you start to see your cash flow increasing every month, once you start to realize you can take control of your financial future, this I promise, you will feel the weight of that stress lifted off your shoulders.

You will feel the debt monkey off your back, and you will experience a renewed enjoyment of life much like it felt when we were little kids growing up.

This is my promise to you.

So start your debt elimination plan and start it today!

* * * * *

"We must be careful not to let our current appetites steal away any chance we might have for a future feast." ... Jim Rohn

Chapter 18
"How to Achieve Financial Independence"

Concept 5 – How to Achieve Financial Independence

Don't you really want to take control of your financial future? Being debt free, with dollars in the bank generating an income stream without having to touch the principal, isn't that really what you want to achieve? Isn't that what achieving financial independence means?

▶ **Fully grasp these next statements.**

Financial independence starts the minute you begin eliminating your debts. Financial independence does not just start after you have paid off all your debts.

Look at it this way.

If you have a credit card on which you pay 18% interest, and you are eliminating that 18% interest debt, then in essence, you are starting your wealth building process.

Also, consider this, would you rather have your money in a bank savings account making you 1% to 3%, or eliminating debt that is costing you 18% or more? That's a no-brainer.

Eliminating debt is by far the best way to use your money.

You start building wealth by eliminating debts.

After you've eliminated all your debts, now it is time to put your money to work for you! And for you in a serious way!

▶ **Pay cash for everything!**

When you want to buy something, then simply save up the money to pay cash. If something costs $500, you pay $500 in cash. You no longer have to charge it on a credit card, and end up paying, for example, $700 for that same item after making interest payments.

▸ Need a new car? **Pay cash!**

▸ Need a new home? **Pay cash!**

▸ Whatever you need, you can now... **PAY CASH!**

No more giving your money away to creditors in the form of interest payments. Seriously, wouldn't you rather pay $500 for a $500 item? Wouldn't you prefer to keep the $200 interest money in your own pocket?

▸ **Here is another statement to fully comprehend.**

You are now spending your current income dollars and not your future income dollars! This is vital to understand. You no longer are paying more than the current cost of the item.

▸ **No longer are you using money you will make "tomorrow" to pay for the items you purchased "yesterday."**

Now you can get compound interest working for you. And to do this, you have to buy assets. What are assets? In a simple word, assets are income producing instruments that work for you. Assets build income for you.

Examples of assets are mutual funds, money market funds, CDs, cash, annuities, and real estate. A financial advisor can offer many others, but this will give you an idea of what we are talking about. As you put more and more money into building your assets, compound interest, as shown in the prior examples, has the potential to make it grow and grow.

I am going to take the liberty to give you one explanation as you consider your asset plan and that is an IRA (individual retirement account). An IRA is one way to save money for the long term. One of the more frequent questions I heard, and typically from younger adults was, "What is a Roth IRA?"

▸ Roth IRA vs. Traditional IRA

Very simply stated, with a Traditional IRA you don't pay taxes on the money as you make periodic deposits into the IRA. A benefit is that it can lower your current taxes.

However, with a Traditional IRA, you pay taxes on the money when you take it out at retirement age. In essence, you are paying taxes on the money you deposited and taxes on the growth of your money. In some cases, one's tax rate is lower at retirement age, so that's another potential benefit of having a Traditional IRA.

▸ Why everyone (in my opinion) should have a Roth.

With a Roth IRA, you pay taxes on the money "before" you make deposits into the IRA. Here is the big benefit of having a Roth IRA; at retirement, when you are taking withdrawals, under most circumstances you pay no taxes on the money you had deposited or on the growth of your money. So, if the total amount of money has grown from factors like compound interest and overall stock market growth, then your nest egg at retirement could go much further because of not having to pay taxes on any of the money in your Roth IRA.

Think about it from this analogy. A farmer can pay taxes on the "seed" or he can pay taxes on the "harvest."

In a Traditional IRA, you pay taxes on the harvest. In a Roth, you pay taxes on the seed but pay no taxes on the harvest. And, the harvest can be significantly greater than the seed.

Now, as you move forward, the objective is to redirect the monies you were spending on debt elimination and now put that money to work for you. This is one way that you can start to build wealth. As your wealth grows, you will reach a point where you can literally live off the interest it produces for you and never have to touch the principal.

Here's one last example of the power of compound interest, time value of money, and consistency.

Imagine this. All your debts are gone. Your house payment is gone. You have $2,000 per month you can now invest for your future. The chart below shows the power of $2,000 invested monthly, with an 8% return, over a 30 year period. In 10 years the value is $368,331; in 20 years the value is $1,185,894, and in 30 years the value is $3,000,590.

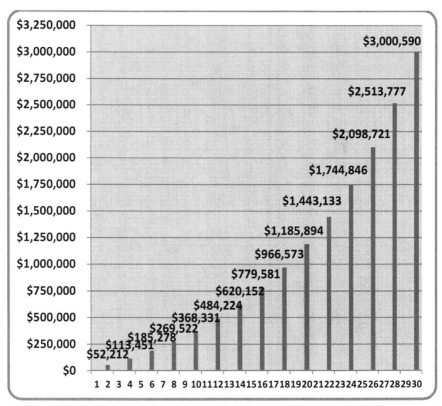

Yes, over 3.0 million dollars. Financial freedom?

I think so! Don't you?

You will reap many benefits by achieving this level of wealth. You'll live a less stressful life. You can live more generously; giving freely. You will know that you will have enough money coming in to pay your living expenses. You will always keep a roof over your head. (And, the reality is, it doesn't take having 3.0 million dollars – it takes being debt free and wise with the money you do make; do have in your account.)

And, you won't end up in the 95% group that is financially wiped out at retirement age. Not to mention all the fun stuff you can do... like taking wonderful vacations, volunteering, and spending more time with family. There are so many benefits to being debt free.

You can choose to start each day with harmony and energy. You can be more involved in your community. Becoming debt free can also create "generational" income; income that will help your family, your children's families, and your grandchildren's families. Being debt free lets you start a new and lasting family legacy! Being debt free lets you craft a vision of your future that is bright, daring, and creative.

As I bring this to a close, my challenge to you is to find the motivation to do what must be done to achieve your financial independence and to live debt free. Find the courage to say "no" to creditors that want every penny you make in your working life.

My wish for you and your family is to be debt free, and by having no debts, you will be less vulnerable. You'll be less vulnerable to economic downturns, upturns, lost jobs, bad bosses, or to other outside financial influences.

Again, I ask you, is today the day you "change just like that?"

How does it feel to be debt free? Well, to be quite honest, it's incredible! I promise you this; as good as you think it will feel to live debt free, **it will be 1,000 times greater.**

However, it's such a personal emotion that it is difficult to adequately express. The feeling of being in control, and not being controlled by others, by creditors, is simply – amazing!

It's something you have to experience for yourself. It's an emotion of accomplishment I hope you will experience in the near future. Just remember to keep the end game in mind and it will come to pass.

▶ **You can change your financial life starting now!**

With the knowledge you have now gained from reading this book, you now hold the knowledge to take control of your time and your financial future!

You can build your road to financial independence! You can live debt free! Take action to start this process for yourself and for your family.

The key is to take action!

In the next chapter, let me share some additional thoughts with you as we look to "pay it forward" for you.

* * * * *

"If you don't design your own life plan, chances are you'll fall into someone else's plan. And guess what they may have planned for you? Not much."

... Jim Rohn

Chapter 19
"One Person Can Make A Difference"

Who are the people in your life that have made a difference?

For me, I've been blessed to have some really special people, a small handful of people, come into my life and influence my future. And what's interesting, is that, at some of those times, I did not even realize the future impact they would have on me.

One person can make a difference!

Gippy Graham is one of those special people. Coach Graham was my high school basketball coach. Did he, and has he, had an influence on me? Oh, yes!

"Coach" came to our high school at the start of my junior year. Now, my problem was that he was my third coach in three years. I say my problem because having three coaches in three years does not create stability. So, by the time Coach arrived, let's just say that I was in need of a little bit of a course correction on the basketball court.

And, Coach provided that leadership and development for me.

As I stated previously, my father passed when I was young. I was blessed to be in a loving home, and my mom was an amazing person; however, I still grew up somewhat fast and somewhat on my own. You could say I was kind of independent. Coach gave me the development, support, guidance, encouragement, and instilled in me something that has stayed with me to this very day.

Coach said, "Nathan, you have to develop a philosophy on life."

To be honest, I didn't fully grasp what he meant at that time. However, as we spent the next two years on the basketball court, and in the classroom, it started to sink in with me. We had many conversations that had nothing to do with basketball but definitely did about life; tremendous learnings.

Coach became the "Father Figure" in my life.

During our time together, Coach said that line to me over and over: "Nathan, you have to develop a philosophy on life." Over the years I have developed a philosophy and part of that is represented in this book.

I greatly appreciate Coach Gippy Graham. He is one of those individuals who really made an impact on my life; so much so, that we have stayed in contact over the years.

Thank you Coach, for paying it forward! **One person can make a difference!**

"I met Nathan a few years ago in Indiana at a gathering for financial advisors. His "get things done" reputation preceded him prior to our meeting, so I was anxious to meet him.

I do not recall what all we discussed during that evening; however, I do recall he told me never to hesitate to contact him, should I ever need anything. Well, after a short time, I indeed took him up on his offer.

Over time of bouncing ideas and theories off of Nathan, I have always marveled at how steady he is. One day, I felt comfortable to ask where his position of financial strength comes from in his life. His answer is something that has never left me.

Joe, he said, "I never again want to be in a position, where someone can put the squeeze on me."

Upon reflection, that one phrase has been a mantra for me ever since he said it that day.

The weight of owing another, be it personal or business, has a ripple effect that many of us do not fully comprehend. It far exceeds just dollars and cents. I know, I've also been there. It becomes a consumption of mental and emotional energy, a distraction of thought and a detour of our momentum. Proverbs 22:7 warns us that "the rich rule over the poor and the borrower is a servant to the lender."

If you are like the majority of Americans who cannot write a $500 check for emergency needs, then may this book serve as a wakeup call. Unfortunately, I see this all too often, as my company advises people on their finances, which always impacts their personal and business goals. However, it is difficult to plan for growth, when we are tethered to consequences of past decisions.

When Nathan said "never again" that tells you that he once was there. He has felt the same fear and pressure that perhaps you may be feeling at this very moment. He simply used the concepts and principles outlined in this book as a key, to de-shackle and overcome.

Now, you are only a decision away, as Nathan invites you to begin your path to financial freedom as he has also helped me, and my family, on our own path to Live Debt Free.

Can one person make a difference? Yes, one person can make a difference; I know, as Nathan is one of those people in my life.

God's best to your new journey."

Joseph O. Fritts

Thank you Joe, for paying it forward! You've openly shared your insights, and kind words, and it is greatly appreciated.

"You must constantly ask yourself these questions: Who am I around? What are they doing to me? What have they got me reading? What have they got me saying? Where do they have me going? What do they have me thinking? And, most important, what do they have me becoming? Then ask yourself the big question: Is that okay?"

... Jim Rohn

So, now allow me to close as we began; with the end in mind.

And the end result is this:

YOU ARE 100% DEBT FREE!

▸ All your debts are paid!

▸ Your home mortgage is paid!

▸ You pay cash for everything!

▸ You are investing money and building real wealth!

You have combined the power of eliminating your debts and getting your money to work for you. With these you have more ownership of your time and are working towards true financial independence!

Ralph Waldo Emerson said, ***"People only see what they are prepared to see."***

Our goal has been to help equip you, and prepare you, to open your eyes, so you can "see" the great potential for your financial future. The greatest forest started from just one small acorn. Take this step-by-step and you will prepare yourself for a life to live debt free! You can change the legacy for your family for generations to come.

Don't let someone else tell you that you cannot do it; just because they have never done it. As we just talked about, position yourself so you can pay it forward. Forward for yourself, forward for your family, and forward for those who you may never know you've even impacted.

Constantly ask yourself the important questions about where you are going, what you want to accomplish, what are you building for the future, and then ask, "Is that okay?"

Can you achieve this on your road to financial independence?

Absolutely!

> ▸ **As motivational speaker Zig Ziglar stated,
> "It was character that got us out of bed,
> commitment that moved us into action, and
> discipline that enabled us to follow through."**

You have been provided a road map and knowledge to live debt free and to achieve financial independence; as you define how it will look for your family and for yourself.

Micah Dixon wrote in his Foreword, *"Folks, this stuff works. If you're serious about improving your financial position, and deleting debt, the steps clearly set forth in this book will empower you to accomplish your goals."* There is no doubt that you are now empowered to live debt free and to achieve your financial freedom.

Act on your character, commitment, and discipline to achieve your goals. For if you will accept these ideas, work hard and continue to persevere, then you are on a collision course with success, and the only variable is time!

I've done it – and so can you!

My story began on July 25th, 1996. Today, your story begins!

Welcome To Your New Beginning!

I Wish You Maximum Success!

Nathan Dickerson

"Vincit Qui Se Vincit"

"How long should you try?

Until.

...Jim Rohn

30 Year Amortization

$200,000 Principal – 7.00% Interest

Event	Date	P&I	Interest	Principal	Balance
Loan	12-01-2005			200,000	
1	01-01-2006	1,330.60	1,166.67	163.93	199,836.07
2	02-01-2006	1,330.60	1,165.71	164.89	199,671.18
3	03-01-2006	1,330.60	1,164.75	165.85	199,505.33
4	04-01-2006	1,330.60	1,163.78	166.82	199,338.51
5	05-01-2006	1,330.60	1,162.81	167.79	199,170.72
6	06-01-2006	1,330.60	1,161.83	168.77	199,001.95
7	07-01-2006	1,330.60	1,160.84	169.76	198,832.19
8	08-01-2006	1,330.60	1,159.85	170.75	198,661.44
9	09-01-2006	1,330.60	1,158.86	171.74	198,489.70
10	10-01-2006	1,330.60	1,157.86	172.74	198,316.96
11	11-01-2006	1,330.60	1,156.85	173.75	198,143.21
12	12-01-2006	1,330.60	1,155.84	174.76	197,968.45
Year 1 Total		**15,967.20**	**13,935.65**	**2,031.55**	
13	01-01-2007	1,330.60	1,154.82	175.78	197,792.67
14	02-01-2007	1,330.60	1,153.79	176.81	197,615.86
15	03-01-2007	1,330.60	1,152.76	177.84	197,438.02
16	04-01-2007	1,330.60	1,151.72	178.88	197,259.14
17	05-01-2007	1,330.60	1,150.68	179.92	197,079.22
18	06-01-2007	1,330.60	1,149.63	180.97	196,898.25
19	07-01-2007	1,330.60	1,148.57	182.03	196,716.22
20	08-01-2007	1,330.60	1,147.51	183.09	196,533.13
21	09-01-2007	1,330.60	1,146.44	184.16	196,348.97
22	10-01-2007	1,330.60	1,145.37	185.23	196,163.74
23	11-01-2007	1,330.60	1,144.29	186.31	195,977.43
24	12-01-2007	1,330.60	1,143.20	187.40	195,790.03
Year 2 Total		**15,967.20**	**13,788.78**	**2,178.42**	
25	01-01-2008	1,330.60	1,142.11	188.49	195,601.54
26	02-01-2008	1,330.60	1,141.01	189.59	195,411.95
27	03-01-2008	1,330.60	1,139.90	190.70	195,221.25
28	04-01-2008	1,330.60	1,138.79	191.81	195,029.44

Event	Date	P&I	Interest	Principal	Balance
29	05-01-2008	1,330.60	1,137.67	192.93	194,836.51
30	06-01-2008	1,330.60	1,136.55	194.05	194,642.46
31	07-01-2008	1,330.60	1,135.41	195.19	194,447.27
32	08-01-2008	1,330.60	1,134.28	196.32	194,250.95
33	09-01-2008	1,330.60	1,133.13	197.47	194,053.48
34	10-01-2008	1,330.60	1,131.98	198.62	193,854.86
35	11-01-2008	1,330.60	1,130.82	199.78	193,655.08
36	12-01-2008	1,330.60	1,129.65	200.95	193,454.13
Year 3 Total		**15,967.20**	**13,631.30**	**2,335.90**	
37	01-01-2009	1,330.60	1,128.48	202.12	193,252.01
38	02-01-2009	1,330.60	1,127.30	203.30	193,048.71
39	03-01-2009	1,330.60	1,126.12	204.48	192,844.23
40	04-01-2009	1,330.60	1,124.92	205.68	192,638.55
41	05-01-2009	1,330.60	1,123.72	206.88	192,431.67
42	06-01-2009	1,330.60	1,122.52	208.08	192,223.59
43	07-01-2009	1,330.60	1,121.30	209.30	192,014.29
44	08-01-2009	1,330.60	1,120.08	210.52	191,803.77
45	09-01-2009	1,330.60	1,118.86	211.74	191,592.03
46	10-01-2009	1,330.60	1,117.62	212.98	191,379.05
47	11-01-2009	1,330.60	1,116.38	214.22	191,164.83
48	12-01-2009	1,330.60	1,115.13	215.47	190,949.36
Year 4 Total		**15,967.20**	**13,462.43**	**2,504.77**	
49	01-01-2010	1,330.60	1,113.87	216.73	190,732.63
50	02-01-2010	1,330.60	1,112.61	217.99	190,514.64
51	03-01-2010	1,330.60	1,111.34	219.26	190,295.38
52	04-01-2010	1,330.60	1,110.06	220.54	190,074.84
53	05-01-2010	1,330.60	1,108.77	221.83	189,853.01
54	06-01-2010	1,330.60	1,107.48	223.12	189,629.89
55	07-01-2010	1,330.60	1,106.17	224.43	189,405.46
56	08-01-2010	1,330.60	1,104.87	225.73	189,179.73
57	09-01-2010	1,330.60	1,103.55	227.05	188,952.68
58	10-01-2010	1,330.60	1,102.22	228.38	188,724.30
59	11-01-2010	1,330.60	1,100.89	229.71	188,494.59
60	12-01-2010	1,330.60	1,099.55	231.05	188,263.54
Year 5 Total		**15,967.20**	**13,281.38**	**2,685.82**	

Event	Date	P&I	Interest	Principal	Balance
61	01-01-2011	1,330.60	1,098.20	232.40	188,031.14
62	02-01-2011	1,330.60	1,096.85	233.75	187,797.39
63	03-01-2011	1,330.60	1,095.48	235.12	187,562.27
64	04-01-2011	1,330.60	1,094.11	236.49	187,325.78
65	05-01-2011	1,330.60	1,092.73	237.87	187,087.91
66	06-01-2011	1,330.60	1,091.35	239.25	186,848.66
67	07-01-2011	1,330.60	1,089.95	240.65	186,608.01
68	08-01-2011	1,330.60	1,088.55	242.05	186,365.96
69	09-01-2011	1,330.60	1,087.13	243.47	186,122.49
70	10-01-2011	1,330.60	1,085.71	244.89	185,877.60
71	11-01-2011	1,330.60	1,084.29	246.31	185,631.29
72	12-01-2011	1,330.60	1,082.85	247.75	185,383.54
Year 6 Total		**15,967.20**	**13,087.20**	**2,880.00**	
73	01-01-2012	1,330.60	1,081.40	249.20	185,134.34
74	02-01-2012	1,330.60	1,079.95	250.65	184,883.69
75	03-01-2012	1,330.60	1,078.49	252.11	184,631.58
76	04-01-2012	1,330.60	1,077.02	253.58	184,378.00
77	05-01-2012	1,330.60	1,075.54	255.06	184,122.94
78	06-01-2012	1,330.60	1,074.05	256.55	183,866.39
79	07-01-2012	1,330.60	1,072.55	258.05	183,608.34
80	08-01-2012	1,330.60	1,071.05	259.55	183,348.79
81	09-01-2012	1,330.60	1,069.53	261.07	183,087.72
82	10-01-2012	1,330.60	1,068.01	262.59	182,825.13
83	11-01-2012	1,330.60	1,066.48	264.12	182,561.01
84	12-01-2012	1,330.60	1,064.94	265.66	182,295.35
Year 7 Total		**15,967.20**	**12,879.01**	**3,088.19**	
85	01-01-2013	1,330.60	1,063.39	267.21	182,028.14
86	02-01-2013	1,330.60	1,061.83	268.77	181,759.37
87	03-01-2013	1,330.60	1,060.26	270.34	181,489.03
88	04-01-2013	1,330.60	1,058.69	271.91	181,217.12
89	05-01-2013	1,330.60	1,057.10	273.50	180,943.62
90	06-01-2013	1,330.60	1,055.50	275.10	180,668.52
91	07-01-2013	1,330.60	1,053.90	276.70	180,391.82
92	08-01-2013	1,330.60	1,052.29	278.31	180,113.51
93	09-01-2013	1,330.60	1,050.66	279.94	179,833.57

Event	Date	P&I	Interest	Principal	Balance
94	10-01-2013	1,330.60	1,049.03	281.57	179,552.00
95	11-01-2013	1,330.60	1,047.39	283.21	179,268.79
96	12-01-2013	1,330.60	1,045.73	284.87	178,983.92
Year 8 Total		15,967.20	12,655.77	3,311.43	
97	01-01-2014	1,330.60	1,044.07	286.53	178,697.39
98	02-01-2014	1,330.60	1,042.40	288.20	178,409.19
99	03-01-2014	1,330.60	1,040.72	289.88	178,119.31
100	04-01-2014	1,330.60	1,039.03	291.57	177,827.74
101	05-01-2014	1,330.60	1,037.33	293.27	177,534.47
102	06-01-2014	1,330.60	1,035.62	294.98	177,239.49
103	07-01-2014	1,330.60	1,033.90	296.70	176,942.79
104	08-01-2014	1,330.60	1,032.17	298.43	176,644.36
105	09-01-2014	1,330.60	1,030.43	300.17	176,344.19
106	10-01-2014	1,330.60	1,028.67	301.93	176,042.26
107	11-01-2014	1,330.60	1,026.91	303.69	175,738.57
108	12-01-2014	1,330.60	1,025.14	305.46	175,433.11
Year 9 Total		15,967.20	12,416.39	3,550.81	
109	01-01-2015	1,330.60	1,023.36	307.24	175,125.87
110	02-01-2015	1,330.60	1,021.57	309.03	174,816.84
111	03-01-2015	1,330.60	1,019.76	310.84	174,506.00
112	04-01-2015	1,330.60	1,017.95	312.65	174,193.35
113	05-01-2015	1,330.60	1,016.13	314.47	173,878.88
114	06-01-2015	1,330.60	1,014.29	316.31	173,562.57
115	07-01-2015	1,330.60	1,012.45	318.15	173,244.42
116	08-01-2015	1,330.60	1,010.59	320.01	172,924.41
117	09-01-2015	1,330.60	1,008.73	321.87	172,602.54
118	10-01-2015	1,330.60	1,006.85	323.75	172,278.79
119	11-01-2015	1,330.60	1,004.96	325.64	171,953.15
120	12-01-2015	1,330.60	1,003.06	327.54	171,625.61
Year 10 Total		15,967.20	12,159.70	3,807.50	
121	01-01-2016	1,330.60	1,001.15	329.45	171,296.16
122	02-01-2016	1,330.60	999.23	331.37	170,964.79
123	03-01-2016	1,330.60	997.29	333.31	170,631.48
124	04-01-2016	1,330.60	995.35	335.25	170,296.23

Event	Date	P&I	Interest	Principal	Balance
125	05-01-2016	1,330.60	993.39	337.21	169,959.02
126	06-01-2016	1,330.60	991.43	339.17	169,619.85
127	07-01-2016	1,330.60	989.45	341.15	169,278.70
128	08-01-2016	1,330.60	987.46	343.14	168,935.56
129	09-01-2016	1,330.60	985.46	345.14	168,590.42
130	10-01-2016	1,330.60	983.44	347.16	168,243.26
131	11-01-2016	1,330.60	981.42	349.18	167,894.08
132	12-01-2016	1,330.60	979.38	351.22	167,542.86
Year 11 Total		**15,967.20**	**11,884.45**	**4,082.75**	
133	01-01-2017	1,330.60	977.33	353.27	167,189.59
134	02-01-2017	1,330.60	975.27	355.33	166,834.26
135	03-01-2017	1,330.60	973.20	357.40	166,476.86
136	04-01-2017	1,330.60	971.12	359.48	166,117.38
137	05-01-2017	1,330.60	969.02	361.58	165,755.80
138	06-01-2017	1,330.60	966.91	363.69	165,392.11
139	07-01-2017	1,330.60	964.79	365.81	165,026.30
140	08-01-2017	1,330.60	962.65	367.95	164,658.35
141	09-01-2017	1,330.60	960.51	370.09	164,288.26
142	10-01-2017	1,330.60	958.35	372.25	163,916.01
143	11-01-2017	1,330.60	956.18	374.42	163,541.59
144	12-01-2017	1,330.60	953.99	376.61	163,164.98
Year 12 Total		**15,967.20**	**11,589.32**	**4,377.88**	
145	01-01-2018	1,330.60	951.80	378.80	162,786.18
146	02-01-2018	1,330.60	949.59	381.01	162,405.17
147	03-01-2018	1,330.60	947.36	383.24	162,021.93
148	04-01-2018	1,330.60	945.13	385.47	161,636.46
149	05-01-2018	1,330.60	942.88	387.72	161,248.74
150	06-01-2018	1,330.60	940.62	389.98	160,858.76
151	07-01-2018	1,330.60	938.34	392.26	160,466.50
152	08-01-2018	1,330.60	936.05	394.55	160,071.95
153	09-01-2018	1,330.60	933.75	396.85	159,675.10
154	10-01-2018	1,330.60	931.44	399.16	159,275.94
155	11-01-2018	1,330.60	929.11	401.49	158,874.45
156	12-01-2018	1,330.60	926.77	403.83	158,470.62
Year 13 Total		**15,967.20**	**11,272.84**	**4,694.36**	

Event	Date	P&I	Interest	Principal	Balance
157	01-01-2019	1,330.60	924.41	406.19	158,064.43
158	02-01-2019	1,330.60	922.04	408.56	157,655.87
159	03-01-2019	1,330.60	919.66	410.94	157,244.93
160	04-01-2019	1,330.60	917.26	413.34	156,831.59
161	05-01-2019	1,330.60	914.85	415.75	156,415.84
162	06-01-2019	1,330.60	912.43	418.17	155,997.67
163	07-01-2019	1,330.60	909.99	420.61	155,577.06
164	08-01-2019	1,330.60	907.53	423.07	155,153.99
165	09-01-2019	1,330.60	905.06	425.54	154,728.45
166	10-01-2019	1,330.60	902.58	428.02	154,300.43
167	11-01-2019	1,330.60	900.09	430.51	153,869.92
168	12-01-2019	1,330.60	897.57	433.03	153,436.89
Year 14 Total		15,967.20	10,933.47	5,033.73	
169	01-01-2020	1,330.60	895.05	435.55	153,001.34
170	02-01-2020	1,330.60	892.51	438.09	152,563.25
171	03-01-2020	1,330.60	889.95	440.65	152,122.60
172	04-01-2020	1,330.60	887.38	443.22	151,679.38
173	05-01-2020	1,330.60	884.80	445.80	151,233.58
174	06-01-2020	1,330.60	882.20	448.40	150,785.18
175	07-01-2020	1,330.60	879.58	451.02	150,334.16
176	08-01-2020	1,330.60	876.95	453.65	149,880.51
177	09-01-2020	1,330.60	874.30	456.30	149,424.21
178	10-01-2020	1,330.60	871.64	458.96	148,965.25
179	11-01-2020	1,330.60	868.96	461.64	148,503.61
180	12-01-2020	1,330.60	866.27	464.33	148,039.28
Year 15 Total		15,967.20	10,569.59	5,397.61	
181	01-01-2021	1,330.60	863.56	467.04	147,572.24
182	02-01-2021	1,330.60	860.84	469.76	147,102.48
183	03-01-2021	1,330.60	858.10	472.50	146,629.98
184	04-01-2021	1,330.60	855.34	475.26	146,154.72
185	05-01-2021	1,330.60	852.57	478.03	145,676.69
186	06-01-2021	1,330.60	849.78	480.82	145,195.87
187	07-01-2021	1,330.60	846.98	483.62	144,712.25
188	08-01-2021	1,330.60	844.15	486.45	144,225.80
189	09-01-2021	1,330.60	841.32	489.28	143,736.52

Event	Date	P&I	Interest	Principal	Balance
190	10-01-2021	1,330.60	838.46	492.14	143,244.38
191	11-01-2021	1,330.60	835.59	495.01	142,749.37
192	12-01-2021	1,330.60	832.70	497.90	142,251.47
Year 16 Total		**15,967.20**	**10,179.39**	**5,787.81**	
193	01-01-2022	1,330.60	829.80	500.80	141,750.67
194	02-01-2022	1,330.60	826.88	503.72	141,246.95
195	03-01-2022	1,330.60	823.94	506.66	140,740.29
196	04-01-2022	1,330.60	820.99	509.61	140,230.68
197	05-01-2022	1,330.60	818.01	512.59	139,718.09
198	06-01-2022	1,330.60	815.02	515.58	139,202.51
199	07-01-2022	1,330.60	812.01	518.59	138,683.92
200	08-01-2022	1,330.60	808.99	521.61	138,162.31
201	09-01-2022	1,330.60	805.95	524.65	137,637.66
202	10-01-2022	1,330.60	802.89	527.71	137,109.95
203	11-01-2022	1,330.60	799.81	530.79	136,579.16
204	12-01-2022	1,330.60	796.71	533.89	136,045.27
Year 17 Total		**15,967.20**	**9,761.00**	**6,206.20**	
205	01-01-2023	1,330.60	793.60	537.00	135,508.27
206	02-01-2023	1,330.60	790.46	540.14	134,968.13
207	03-01-2023	1,330.60	787.31	543.29	134,424.84
208	04-01-2023	1,330.60	784.14	546.46	133,878.38
209	05-01-2023	1,330.60	780.96	549.64	133,328.74
210	06-01-2023	1,330.60	777.75	552.85	132,775.89
211	07-01-2023	1,330.60	774.53	556.07	132,219.82
212	08-01-2023	1,330.60	771.28	559.32	131,660.50
213	09-01-2023	1,330.60	768.02	562.58	131,097.92
214	10-01-2023	1,330.60	764.74	565.86	130,532.06
215	11-01-2023	1,330.60	761.44	569.16	129,962.90
216	12-01-2023	1,330.60	758.12	572.48	129,390.42
Year 18 Total		**15,967.20**	**9,312.35**	**6,654.85**	
217	01-01-2024	1,330.60	754.78	575.82	128,814.60
218	02-01-2024	1,330.60	751.42	579.18	128,235.42
219	03-01-2024	1,330.60	748.04	582.56	127,652.86
220	04-01-2024	1,330.60	744.64	585.96	127,066.90

Event	Date	P&I	Interest	Principal	Balance
221	05-01-2024	1,330.60	741.22	589.38	126,477.52
222	06-01-2024	1,330.60	737.79	592.81	125,884.71
223	07-01-2024	1,330.60	734.33	596.27	125,288.44
224	08-01-2024	1,330.60	730.85	599.75	124,688.69
225	09-01-2024	1,330.60	727.35	603.25	124,085.44
226	10-01-2024	1,330.60	723.83	606.77	123,478.67
227	11-01-2024	1,330.60	720.29	610.31	122,868.36
228	12-01-2024	1,330.60	716.73	613.87	122,254.49
Year 19 Total		**15,967.20**	**8,831.27**	**7,135.93**	
229	01-01-2025	1,330.60	713.15	617.45	121,637.04
230	02-01-2025	1,330.60	709.55	621.05	121,015.99
231	03-01-2025	1,330.60	705.93	624.67	120,391.32
232	04-01-2025	1,330.60	702.28	628.32	119,763.00
233	05-01-2025	1,330.60	698.62	631.98	119,131.02
234	06-01-2025	1,330.60	694.93	635.67	118,495.35
235	07-01-2025	1,330.60	691.22	639.38	117,855.97
236	08-01-2025	1,330.60	687.49	643.11	117,212.86
237	09-01-2025	1,330.60	683.74	646.86	116,566.00
238	10-01-2025	1,330.60	679.97	650.63	115,915.37
239	11-01-2025	1,330.60	676.17	654.43	115,260.94
240	12-01-2025	1,330.60	672.36	658.24	114,602.70
Year 20 Total		**15,967.20**	**8,315.41**	**7,651.79**	
241	01-01-2026	1,330.60	668.52	662.08	113,940.62
242	02-01-2026	1,330.60	664.65	665.95	113,274.67
243	03-01-2026	1,330.60	660.77	669.83	112,604.84
244	04-01-2026	1,330.60	656.86	673.74	111,931.10
245	05-01-2026	1,330.60	652.93	677.67	111,253.43
246	06-01-2026	1,330.60	648.98	681.62	110,571.81
247	07-01-2026	1,330.60	645.00	685.60	109,886.21
248	08-01-2026	1,330.60	641.00	689.60	109,196.61
249	09-01-2026	1,330.60	636.98	693.62	108,502.99
250	10-01-2026	1,330.60	632.93	697.67	107,805.32
251	11-01-2026	1,330.60	628.86	701.74	107,103.58
252	12-01-2026	1,330.60	624.77	705.83	106,397.75
Year 21 Total		**15,967.20**	**7,762.25**	**8,204.95**	

Event	Date	P&I	Interest	Principal	Balance
253	01-01-2027	1,330.60	620.65	709.95	105,687.80
254	02-01-2027	1,330.60	616.51	714.09	104,973.71
255	03-01-2027	1,330.60	612.35	718.25	104,255.46
256	04-01-2027	1,330.60	608.16	722.44	103,533.02
257	05-01-2027	1,330.60	603.94	726.66	102,806.36
258	06-01-2027	1,330.60	599.70	730.90	102,075.46
259	07-01-2027	1,330.60	595.44	735.16	101,340.30
260	08-01-2027	1,330.60	591.15	739.45	100,600.85
261	09-01-2027	1,330.60	586.84	743.76	99,857.09
262	10-01-2027	1,330.60	582.50	748.10	99,108.99
263	11-01-2027	1,330.60	578.14	752.46	98,356.53
264	12-01-2027	1,330.60	573.75	756.85	97,599.68
Year 22 Total		15,967.20	7,169.13	8,798.07	
265	01-01-2028	1,330.60	569.33	761.27	96,838.41
266	02-01-2028	1,330.60	564.89	765.71	96,072.70
267	03-01-2028	1,330.60	560.42	770.18	95,302.52
268	04-01-2028	1,330.60	555.93	774.67	94,527.85
269	05-01-2028	1,330.60	551.41	779.19	93,748.66
270	06-01-2028	1,330.60	546.87	783.73	92,964.93
271	07-01-2028	1,330.60	542.30	788.30	92,176.63
272	08-01-2028	1,330.60	537.70	792.90	91,383.73
273	09-01-2028	1,330.60	533.07	797.53	90,586.20
274	10-01-2028	1,330.60	528.42	802.18	89,784.02
275	11-01-2028	1,330.60	523.74	806.86	88,977.16
276	12-01-2028	1,330.60	519.03	811.57	88,165.59
Year 23 Total		15,967.20	6,533.11	9,434.09	
277	01-01-2029	1,330.60	514.30	816.30	87,349.29
278	02-01-2029	1,330.60	509.54	821.06	86,528.23
279	03-01-2029	1,330.60	504.75	825.85	85,702.38
280	04-01-2029	1,330.60	499.93	830.67	84,871.71
281	05-01-2029	1,330.60	495.08	835.52	84,036.19
282	06-01-2029	1,330.60	490.21	840.39	83,195.80
283	07-01-2029	1,330.60	485.31	845.29	82,350.51
284	08-01-2029	1,330.60	480.38	850.22	81,500.29
285	09-01-2029	1,330.60	475.42	855.18	80,645.11

Event	Date	P&I	Interest	Principal	Balance
286	10-01-2029	1,330.60	470.43	860.17	79,784.94
287	11-01-2029	1,330.60	465.41	865.19	78,919.75
288	12-01-2029	1,330.60	460.37	870.23	78,049.52
Year 24 Total		**15,967.20**	**5,851.13**	**10,116.07**	
289	01-01-2030	1,330.60	455.29	875.31	77,174.21
290	02-01-2030	1,330.60	450.18	880.42	76,293.79
291	03-01-2030	1,330.60	445.05	885.55	75,408.24
292	04-01-2030	1,330.60	439.88	890.72	74,517.52
293	05-01-2030	1,330.60	434.69	895.91	73,621.61
294	06-01-2030	1,330.60	429.46	901.14	72,720.47
295	07-01-2030	1,330.60	424.20	906.40	71,814.07
296	08-01-2030	1,330.60	418.92	911.68	70,902.39
297	09-01-2030	1,330.60	413.60	917.00	69,985.39
298	10-01-2030	1,330.60	408.25	922.35	69,063.04
299	11-01-2030	1,330.60	402.87	927.73	68,135.31
300	12-01-2030	1,330.60	397.46	933.14	67,202.17
Year 25 Total		**15,967.20**	**5,119.85**	**10,847.35**	
301	01-01-2031	1,330.60	392.01	938.59	66,263.58
302	02-01-2031	1,330.60	386.54	944.06	65,319.52
303	03-01-2031	1,330.60	381.03	949.57	64,369.95
304	04-01-2031	1,330.60	375.49	955.11	63,414.84
305	05-01-2031	1,330.60	369.92	960.68	62,454.16
306	06-01-2031	1,330.60	364.32	966.28	61,487.88
307	07-01-2031	1,330.60	358.68	971.92	60,515.96
308	08-01-2031	1,330.60	353.01	977.59	59,538.37
309	09-01-2031	1,330.60	347.31	983.29	58,555.08
310	10-01-2031	1,330.60	341.57	989.03	57,566.05
311	11-01-2031	1,330.60	335.80	994.80	56,571.25
312	12-01-2031	1,330.60	330.00	1,000.60	55,570.65
Year 26 Total		**15,967.20**	**4,335.68**	**11,631.52**	
313	01-01-2032	1,330.60	324.16	1,006.44	54,564.21
314	02-01-2032	1,330.60	318.29	1,012.31	53,551.90
315	03-01-2032	1,330.60	312.39	1,018.21	52,533.69
316	04-01-2032	1,330.60	306.45	1,024.15	51,509.54

Event	Date	P&I	Interest	Principal	Balance
317	05-01-2032	1,330.60	300.47	1,030.13	50,479.41
318	06-01-2032	1,330.60	294.46	1,036.14	49,443.27
319	07-01-2032	1,330.60	288.42	1,042.18	48,401.09
320	08-01-2032	1,330.60	282.34	1,048.26	47,352.83
321	09-01-2032	1,330.60	276.22	1,054.38	46,298.45
322	10-01-2032	1,330.60	270.07	1,060.53	45,237.92
323	11-01-2032	1,330.60	263.89	1,066.71	44,171.21
324	12-01-2032	1,330.60	257.67	1,072.93	43,098.28
Year 27 Total		**15,967.20**	**3,494.83**	**12,472.37**	
325	01-01-2033	1,330.60	251.41	1,079.19	42,019.09
326	02-01-2033	1,330.60	245.11	1,085.49	40,933.60
327	03-01-2033	1,330.60	238.78	1,091.82	39,841.78
328	04-01-2033	1,330.60	232.41	1,098.19	38,743.59
329	05-01-2033	1,330.60	226.00	1,104.60	37,638.99
330	06-01-2033	1,330.60	219.56	1,111.04	36,527.95
331	07-01-2033	1,330.60	213.08	1,117.52	35,410.43
332	08-01-2033	1,330.60	206.56	1,124.04	34,286.39
333	09-01-2033	1,330.60	200.00	1,130.60	33,155.79
334	10-01-2033	1,330.60	193.41	1,137.19	32,018.60
335	11-01-2033	1,330.60	186.78	1,143.82	30,874.78
336	12-01-2033	1,330.60	180.10	1,150.50	29,724.28
Year 28 Total		**15,967.20**	**2,593.20**	**13,374.00**	
337	01-01-2034	1,330.60	173.39	1,157.21	28,567.07
338	02-01-2034	1,330.60	166.64	1,163.96	27,403.11
339	03-01-2034	1,330.60	159.85	1,170.75	26,232.36
340	04-01-2034	1,330.60	153.02	1,177.58	25,054.78
341	05-01-2034	1,330.60	146.15	1,184.45	23,870.33
342	06-01-2034	1,330.60	139.24	1,191.36	22,678.97
343	07-01-2034	1,330.60	132.29	1,198.31	21,480.66
344	08-01-2034	1,330.60	125.30	1,205.30	20,275.36
345	09-01-2034	1,330.60	118.27	1,212.33	19,063.03
346	10-01-2034	1,330.60	111.20	1,219.40	17,843.63
347	11-01-2034	1,330.60	104.09	1,226.51	16,617.12
348	12-01-2034	1,330.60	96.93	1,233.67	15,383.45
Year 29 Total		**15,967.20**	**1,626.37**	**14,340.83**	

Event	Date	P&I	Interest	Principal	Balance
349	01-01-2035	1,330.60	89.74	1,240.86	14,142.59
350	02-01-2035	1,330.60	82.50	1,248.10	12,894.49
351	03-01-2035	1,330.60	75.22	1,255.38	11,639.11
352	04-01-2035	1,330.60	67.89	1,262.71	10,376.40
353	05-01-2035	1,330.60	60.53	1,270.07	9,106.33
354	06-01-2035	1,330.60	53.12	1,277.48	7,828.85
355	07-01-2035	1,330.60	45.67	1,284.93	6,543.92
356	08-01-2035	1,330.60	38.17	1,292.43	5,251.49
357	09-01-2035	1,330.60	30.63	1,299.97	3,951.52
358	10-01-2035	1,330.60	23.05	1,307.55	2,643.97
359	11-01-2035	1,330.60	15.42	1,315.18	1,328.79
360	12-01-2035	1,336.54	7.75	1,322.85	0.00
Year 30 Total		**15,973.14**	**589.69**	**15,377.51**	

| Grand Total | | $479,021.94 | $279,021.94 | | |

"When the promise is clear, the price gets easy."

... Jim Rohn

LIVE DEBT FREE

Made in the USA
Lexington, KY
25 November 2019